IT'S A LONDON THING

FRED BUTLER

IT'S A LONDON THING

AN INSIDER'S CITY GUIDE

PRESTEL
Munich • London • New York

Contents

Bubbles over St Paul's Cathedral from Tate Modern..

Introduction

It's a London thing. It's a glorious thing. It's potentially, at times, a wet and grey thing. But it's also a multicoloured, multifaceted, multicultural multi-pass to something magic. This book contains my insider's insights from a cosmic perspective, and is preoccupied with discovering every detail. It's a guide for navigating the streets—what the local taxi drivers refer to as 'The Knowledge'—and a time capsule that locks in what might later be lost.

The listings in *It's a London Thing* are organised by neighbourhood (Central, North, East, South and West) and each area features a map pinpointing the locations of my recommendations. Every chapter begins with a photograph taken inside my house, providing a sneak peek into my own personal London style. I've also asked a number of the capital's essential idiosyncratic characters for their top tips to bring you a complete 360-degree scoop of the city's flavour.

During my time compiling this compendium I've witnessed cavities being dug out and a canopy of high-rises bionically shoot up. The skyline has fluctuated as quickly as the columns of a volume display rise and fall. Artists' warehouse studios are now a flicker of PC screensavers between partitioned walls. Gentrification is the dirty word on everyone's lips. Our local high streets are becoming high roads and we're having to do a Dick Whittington and dart out of here, to duck and dive to survive.

So here is an antidote to that spiralling fear. Reacquaint yourself with, rediscover and rejoice in what is quintessentially London. Switch off and check in.

Christina Mackie's 2015 Tate Britain Commission, *The Filters.*

Don't go for the pre-packaged 'meal deal' aisle; go into the Italian café that's been here since day dot and have a chat for a more nourishing exchange—and leave with more change. Don't get run down; run along the South Bank at night and see the lights reflect on the lapping Thames like a 21st-century Turner. Run into the National Gallery to see his original bequest paintings for free. Reignite your intrigue with firework displays on Guy Fawkes Night and Diwali. Light your lantern at Chinatown's New Year's parade and your Christingle candle while carol singing at St Paul's. Find a furry friend to hug at a city farm and swim with swans in the Serpentine come summertime. Sunbathe at Hampstead's ponds; let your dog loose and fly a kite at the summit of Parliament Hill Fields. See the skyline from the South Side at Bold Tendencies, Peckham's multi-storey sculpture park. Snuffle out samples of truffle burgers at Borough Market and learn body-popping 'n' locking in the Charing Cross subway. Skate at the Southbank Centre's undercroft and follow the boom-box beats to catch the street dancers practising routines in the first-floor foyer. Hot-desk from the British Library and learn how to service your own wheels at the London Bike Kitchen. Go for a bike ride and stalk some deer with the dappled Bambis in Richmond Park. Plant trees, catch swarms and collect urban honey with Bootstrap Bees.

Chloe Dewe Mathews's 2015 video installation *Congregation* at Bosse & Baum in Peckham, South London.

Artist Bethan Laura Wood at Dover Street Market, a unique London talent
in a unique London space.

Paint your face with flowers for Halloween at the British Museum's Day of the Dead.
Take your date to a Friday Late at the Tate and wait outside Wimbledon for someone
to liberate their day pass to world-class tennis.

      Don't pass up opportunities. Ask questions, beat down doors and don't be
shy. Leave no stone unturned and turn over a new leaf in the way you view London.
Our London. My London … which is now, in turn, your London too. As you turn over
this page, feel the paper and feel the force. Enjoy it. Digest it. Breathe it all in. Exhale
to spread the words of optimistic energy and let the ripples hit the Thames Barrier
and bounce right back again. In the words of Scott Garcia and MC Styles' classic UK
garage tune: *It's. A. London. Thing. This is a London thing.*

Fred Butler
London, 2016

The 100 Club

If you've heard that Ronnie Scott's is the definitive destination for jazz lovers in London, then check out the story of the 100 Club. Founded as a swing club in 1942, it gave US soldiers a place to jitterbug at a time when the dance wasn't widely tolerated. Muddy Waters, B.B. King and Louis Armstrong all played here, which cemented its status as the blues scene's epicentre in the country. As genres shifted through the years, the basement space welcomed Mods in the 1960s and punk and reggae fans in the 1970s before starting its legendary Northern Soul all-nighters in the 1980s. All of these classic moments have been captured and reincarnated as a gallery of photographic prints around the venue. I've hung around after gigs just to take time to look at them all. We're lucky to still be able to see acts play intimate secret shows in this tiny Soho club because, in 2011, it was saved from possible closure after a public fundraising campaign—ultimately, Converse stepped in (forgive the pun) to foot the bill (and another, sorry).

100 Oxford Street, W1D 1LL
the100club.co.uk

Japan Centre Food Hall

The freshest, cheapest, most authentic and extensive selection of sushi boxes you'll find for lunch in London. If you have seen the documentary *Jiro Dreams of Sushi* and come to a higher understanding of the craft that goes into creating these dishes, you'll do well to give the supermarket dregs a wide berth. Dive into the Japan Centre's food hall deli aisles for unrivalled sushi, bento, hot souzai snacks, bakery items and puds. You can also pick up fresh ingredients to take home for dinner and stock up on sake, cute kawaii stationery and sweets. Who doesn't need a heart-shaped sandwich cutter in their life?!

19 Shaftesbury Avenue, W1D 7ED
japancentre.com

BOOM Cycle

For visitors to the city missing their bike back home or Londoners keen to clock up extra miles, BOOM Cycle is the best spin joint in town. Its USP is all about moving to the beat so you're dancing in your seat. Music is at the core of their classes via the playlists selected by their instructors and the stellar audio system installed for a surround sound experience. The lights are low to add to the ambience and encourage shy gym bunnies who prefer to work out under the radar. Bikes are mounted on stadium-like steps so that everyone can see the instructor and join in without getting left behind. After the session, there's a shower block stocked with REN products and fluffy towels so you can turn around Superman-style to leave refreshed and ready to go.

Holborn: 16 Procter Street, WC1V 6NX
Shoreditch: 2–8 Scrutton Street, EC2A 4RT
boomcycle.co.uk

Swim Dem Crew's Christmas swim at Oasis's rooftop pool.

Oasis Sports Centre

Arguably THE most central suntrap and swimming pool in London, Oasis Sports Centre has both an inside and an outside pool on its Covent Garden roof. The al fresco lido is surrounded by a sun deck, providing local workers an insanely luxurious lunch-hour getaway. It's one of Camden Council's best kept secrets. Until now. Sorry about that, sun-worshippers and swimmers of WC2.

32 Endell Street, WC2H 9AG
better.org.uk/leisure/oasis-sports-centre

Serpentine Lido

Here is the central fresh open-water swimming alternative to North London's Hampstead Heath ponds. Serpentine Lido is an area carved out of Hyde Park's lake, complete with resident swans, geese and ducks. Open during the summer months, it has a terrace of sun loungers and deck chairs for much-needed English seasonal sunbathing. There's also a children's paddling pool to take care of your shoal while you socialise.

Hyde Park, W2 2UH
serpentinelido.com

Regent's Park

Regent's Park is a serene sanctuary within spitting distance of Oxford Circus. Pass the embassies and BBC buildings of Portland Place and you're immediately within the gates of the ridiculously beautiful Queen Mary's Gardens. Four hundred varieties of roses are pruned to perfection in the most idyllic English picture-postcard setting. If a couple of bluebirds paused to kiss in the spectrum mist of the fountain and a bristling bumblebee shook glitter pollen in your path, it wouldn't seem amiss. We're so spoilt with this pocket of paradise that spans from Central to North London; you can take the scenic route through this expanse. It's split into two inner and outer circles where cyclists congregate in the early hours of the morning to race laps before the taxis awake. There are many other sports facilities on offer too, including tennis, netball, athletics, cricket, rounders, football, hockey, rugby, softball, Frisbee and even shinty. For leisurely romantic pursuits, there's boating on the lake alongside the 100 species of waterfowl, just a waddle away from the Snowdon Aviary of London Zoo. That's right: Regent's Park is also home to one of the world's oldest zoos, which in addition runs a scientific research institute and conservation charity. You can either pay the fee for entry or saunter around the hedged edges to catch a glimpse of the giraffes, camels or reindeer, all visible via stealth snooping. You can even hear the roar of the lions all the way from Camden (according to my mum—factually, could be unfounded).

Regent's Park, NW1 4RY
royalparks.org.uk/parks/the-regents-park
zsl.org/zsl-london-zoo

Gary Webb's *Dreamy Bathroom* at Frieze Art Fair's Sculpture Park, 2014.

Prince Charles Cinema

The Prince Charles Cinema, more commonly known as 'the PCC', is on the Leicester Square patch—but isn't in any shape or form comparable to its neighbours. It's a complete one-off and will give you a night you'll never forget. The last time I went, *Taxi Driver* started playing but the audience were too polite to pipe up that the projectionist had popped on the wrong canister, because we'd come to see *Northern Soul*.

      The PCC is what's known as a repertory cinema for its programme of classic and cult celluloid greats; to this end, it shows real film reels in preference to digital. Once upon a time it was one of Soho's porn cinemas but, since undergoing a rebrand as a sing-along cinema, the only suspenders you'll be seeing will be at a screening of *The Rocky Horror Picture Show*. Whatever picture you do pick, pound to a penny it will be one of the cheapest tickets in town. The staff pride themselves on working hard to keep the low prices in place as much as the fun atmosphere and audience participation. If you're one for loud conversation and throwing popcorn, this is the one spot where you won't get anyone spinning round to shush you. Warning: make sure not to plunder your goody bag before the special feature films start. Each toy/sweet is a carefully selected prop to be used (ingested) at key points of the plot.

7 Leicester Place, WC2H 7BY
princecharlescinema.com

Curzon Mayfair

This London cinema franchise is one of the capital's favourite choices. Because it's situated in the snazzy Mayfair neighbourhood, there's an unwritten dress code—so firstly, leave your sneakers at home and, secondly, absolutely *no* feet on the seats!

38 Curzon Street, W1J 7TY
curzoncinemas.com/cinemas/mayfair

Helen Storey, *Red Fur Implantation Dress*, 1997.

Wellcome Collection Reading Room

Situated on the Westway, the main road that runs behind town, is the Wellcome Collection, with its window displays of medical-inspired art installations. Beside the ingenious permanent and temporary exhibitions is a public library, with curated artworks among the literature. Cosy up on a beanbag chair to get your head down for uninterrupted bookworming.

183 Euston Road, NW1 2BE
wellcomecollection.org/readingroom

Claire de Rouen Books

Charing Cross Road is the district for bookshops and thus a destination for bookworms. For years one store stood out not just for its artists' monographs, but for the owner's exceptional presence (and her hilarious sneezy black pug). The shop was Zwemmers and the woman was Claire de Rouen. She had previously worked at the ICA and the Photographers' Gallery before going on to open her own eponymous shop and gallery in 2005. Sadly, she passed away in 2012, but her legacy continues. Model Lily Cole is now a co-owner who occasionally moonlights a shift in the store.

      Claire was friends with the photographers of her generation, such as David Bailey and Bruce Weber, and arranged to stock collectors' items such as special limited editions, signed copies and prints. Equally, she invested time in new talent such as Tyrone Lebon and Valerie Phillips by arranging shows and events. A programme of activities is crucial to the operations of this specialist photography, fashion and beauty bookshop, so check the diary for dates.

First Floor, 125 Charing Cross Road, WC2H 0EW
clairederouenbooks.com

Top 5 Museums & Galleries

Amber Butchart

Amber is like a cartoon superhero come to life, with her exquisite heart-shaped red hair and trademark turban holding in a brain full of academic superpowers. She is an author, lecturer, broadcaster and authority on fashion history, as well as a DJ on the decks as one half of The Broken Hearts. She's also in a perpetual game of musical chairs, hosting or sitting on panel discussions on cultural issues. Here, she shares her favourite London museums and galleries, from Freemasonry to foundlings and fans.

1 The Library and Museum of Freemasonry

'Freemasons' Hall is one of my favourite buildings. Its Art Deco grandeur really has to be seen to be believed. The museum holds a collection of papers and paraphernalia, which is fascinating as there is still so much myth surrounding the Freemasons in popular culture. And they have a shop where you can buy Masonic ties and socks! I love it.' 60 Great Queen Street, WC2B 5AZ freemasonry.london.museum

2 Old Operating Theatre Museum and Herb Garret

'This is a real hidden gem. It houses the oldest operating theatre in Europe and has an old herb garret dating back to the early 18th century, which was used by St Thomas's apothecary to create medicines. It houses a cornucopia of medical artefacts surrounded by herbs and distilling equipment. It's a really unique look into the past.' 9a St Thomas Street, SE1 9RY thegarret.org.uk

3 Sir John Soane's Museum

'Sir John Soane was an architect who demolished and rebuilt three houses starting around the turn of the 19th century. He used the space to live in but also to house his collection of antiquities and architectural oddities; it eventually became known as the "Academy of Architecture". He even managed to negotiate an Act of Parliament to preserve the space as a museum after his death.' 13 Lincoln's Inn Fields, WC2A 3BP soane.org

4 The Foundling Museum

'The Foundling Museum was established in 1739 as a hospital for the "Maintenance and Education of Exposed and Deserted Young Children" (the institution exists today as the Coram children's charity). In an age of philanthropy with no welfare state, it played an important role, and the fashionable upper classes were keen to offer their patronage. William Hogarth was a governor and donated paintings to be displayed. He encouraged others to do the same, which effectively turned the Foundling Hospital into England's first public art gallery.' 40 Brunswick Square, WC1N 1AZ foundlingmuseum.org.uk

5 Fan Museum

'The first museum dedicated to fans has examples from all over the world dating back to the 12th century. The temporary exhibitions and permanent collection tell disparate and intricate stories of many of these items throughout history. The museum has gorgeous Georgian surroundings, as it's located in two houses that were built in the 1720s.' 12 Crooms Hill, SE10 8ER thefanmuseum.org.uk

Amber at Sir John Soane's Museum.

Fashion Space Gallery

In among the plethora of galleries in the centre of town this is perhaps the most central, tucked into the campus of the London College of Fashion behind Oxford Circus. The LCF opened its doors to the public in 2010. Shows are a mixture of work by leading art practitioners and cutting-edge, emerging talent. The space's programming has taken shape through themed group shows, performances and installations with additional events, artist talks and lectures. Exhibitions here have featured or focused on the art of millinery, eyewear, Jean Paul Gaultier, Simon Costin and Yohji Yamamoto. To get a taste for what's in store, just have a look at the window display in reception, which acts as a portal to the show and a secondary installation space.

20 John Princes Street, W1G 0BJ
fashionspacegallery.com

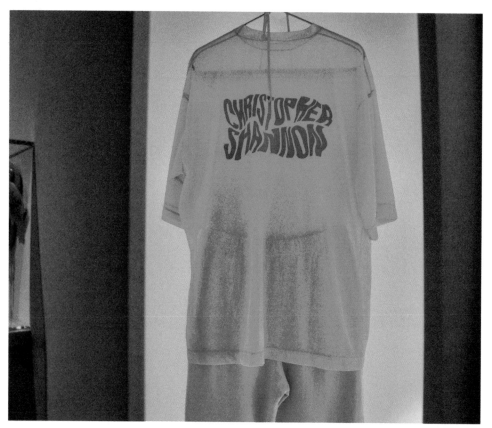

Christopher Shannon's Spring 2016 collection in the 'Mad About the Boy' exhibition.

Performance artist Marvin Gaye Chetwynd's 'insanity workout' at Wright & Vandame's *fig-2* solo exhibition, 2015.

Institute of Contemporary Arts

If you want to kill two birds with one stone (more aptly *pigeons*, given the vicinity!) and visit a London main attraction and a cultural hotspot in one go, this is the place. The ICA is situated at the mouth of the Mall so you can dip in on your way to see the Changing of the Guard at Buckingham Palace. Despite being surrounded by architectural grandeur, it is the perfect modern twist with which to end a visit to the adjacent National Gallery on Trafalgar Square. Exhibitions showcase new, emerging, radical art with the annual Bloomberg New Contemporaries competition.

Collaborations are key to the gallery's programming, especially in making use of its auditorium space for dance and music-related events. Here, ravers rub shoulders with film buffs, as the ICA also houses a cinema for art-related releases. Backing up these brilliant events is a superbly stocked bookshop previously guest curated by Marc Jacobs' Bookmarc and Louis Vuitton Maison's Librarie. It also acts as a gallery shop, selling limited-edition works. One weekend the centre celebrated the legacy of Leigh Bowery with DJ, visual artist and archivist Jeffrey Hinton unveiling original 1980s London nightclub footage before a party dedicated to the scene.

The Mall, SW1Y 5AH
ica.org.uk

Somerset House

I would need a chapter dedicated solely to Somerset House to do it justice. It doesn't actually matter what's going on at any given time, as a visit to see this Neoclassical building on the Thames is a treat in itself. You can enjoy a coffee in the sunshine on its terrace over the river or by the fountain in its main feature—the courtyard. Built on the site of a Tudor palace, this regal arena has a seasonally alternating calendar of attractions, from ice-skating at Christmas to open-air concerts and cinema in the summer. It was once home to London Fashion Week and style has a strong foothold here, with the British Fashion Council's offices in the wings and selected designers' studios in the vaults. The exhibitions are often style-themed and coincide with LFW shows. Previous highlights have included Tim Walker, SHOWstudio, Isabella Blow, Guy Bourdin and Wool Week, which saw the courtyard fenced in, with colour-coated sheep creating a mini city farm!

Aside from its strength in representing contemporary artwork, such as at the 1:54 African Art Fair, Somerset House is notable for its Courtauld Gallery, which displays Old Master and Impressionist paintings. It's important to not overlook this as you're hurried through the gauntlet of paps at the Fashion Week gates, like a gladiator entering the arena.

Somerset House is so close to Covent Garden that I think it's the perfect spot in which to exit the regular tourist scrum and grab a moment's sanctuary in its epic setting. Get lost in its galleries of historical assets and modern art and its Rizzoli Bookshop and fuel up at one of its three eateries. One of my best ever picnic moments was here, having a coronation chicken sandwich and cava on the terrace while waving to the Queen as she sailed down the river on her Diamond Jubilee.

Strand, WC2R 1LA
somersethouse.org.uk

Skate at Somerset House with Fortnum & Mason, 2015.

Portrait of Don Letts in the 'Return of the Rudeboy' exhibition at Somerset House curated by Harris Elliott and Dean Chalkley, 2014.

The Photographers' Gallery

Now based in a purpose-built five-floor home right behind Oxford Street, the Photographers' Gallery was established in 1971 as the first independent gallery in Britain purely to showcase the medium of photography when nowhere else would take it seriously. The gallery also acts as a resource with an onsite archive and study room. For those with more limited time, there's a banging bookshop and café that provide alternative options to the West End's chains. If you leave feeling inspired to put down your smartphone and pick up a proper DSLR, you're in the right area! Nip round the corner to Tottenham Court Road's row of digital stores and then book yourself on a day course at TPG and start recording your own personal history.

16–18 Ramillies Street, W1F 7LW
thephotographersgallery.org.uk

Celebrating Trinidad: a moko jumbie performance by TouchDSky stilt-walkers, 2015.

British Museum

I'm going to have to be honest here: as much as I love appreciating ancient art, I would ideally prefer to experience it in its original context. I feel unreasonably responsible for my nation pilfering the rest of the world's heritage to rehouse it on our own tiny island. That said, once you've wandered past the obelisk on the river to get here, the extent of the Egyptian, Greek and Roman collections on display is incredible. The British Museum was the first national public museum in the world, founded in 1753 and granting free admission. It provides a tour of ancient history without having to leave WC1, with galleries showing highlights from Africa, Antarctica, Asia, Europe, North and Central America, Oceania and South America. In addition to the permanent collection (originally bequeathed by Sir Hans Soane) there are temporary shows—for example, Turner Prize-winner Grayson Perry plundered the archives to piece together his 'The Tomb of the Unknown Craftsman' show in 2011–12.

Great Russell Street, WC1B 3DG
britishmuseum.org

National Gallery

This is it. This is the biggie. And … it's FREE! The National Gallery houses the national collection of 13th–19th-century paintings belonging to the public and therefore does not charge for entry. It's ours! It's iconic. It's vital. And it's geographically totally central, so has the easiest address to find. Follow any London pigeon and you'll probably end up on the head of one of the lion statues out front on Trafalgar Square. Here, you will also find the capital's most prominent piece of public art in the form of the Fourth Plinth. This empty plinth hosts constantly changing pieces by artists who join the lineage of the likes of Rachel Whiteread, Marc Quinn, Antony Gormley, Yinka Shonibare and David Shrigley.

Trafalgar Square, WC2N 5DN
nationalgallery.org.uk

National Portrait Gallery
St Martin's Place, WC2H 0HE
npg.org.uk

Royal Academy
Burlington House, Piccadilly, W1J 0BD
royalacademy.org.uk

You can while away many hours wandering around the National Gallery's collection.

Jim Lambie's stairs for the Summer Exhibition at the Royal Academy, 2015.

Top 5 Countercultural Figures

Princess Julia

Legend has it that the illustrious Princess Julia has been out every night since 1977. A makeup artist in her teens, she became a muse for every iconoclastic London designer, from Stephen Jones in the 1970s to Peter Jensen's 'Julia' Autumn/Winter 2015 collection. The red fingernails that painted the snake across skin in Visage's 1980 music video for 'Fade to Grey' were her own 'actual hands' (in her own words), while her own actual visage has led campaigns for Illamasqua and Space NK. Her cupid's-bow red lips could tell 1,000 stories about dancefloors and DJ decks from the era of punk, to the New Romantic movement, to the origins of rave. She's seen it all but is inexplicably unjaded and eternally eager to show face and support her cross-generation creative friends. From her position FROW at Fashion Week she reports for the likes of Condé Nast, while from the smoking area of nightclub Vogue Fabrics she sees behind the smoke and mirrors of the fashion industry and into the designers' real lives. Here, she lists her top five favourite London countercultural figures.

1 Jonny Woo

'Jonny explores performance mainly via drag. His humorous and poignant shows have inspired and continued to inspire those that witness his repartee. He is also part of the team that own The Glory, a performance pub like no other.'
281 Kingsland Road, E2 8AS
theglory.com

2 Stephen Jones

'I met Stephen in the late 1970s. He was studying fashion but decided to pour his energies into reinventing the hat-making world. Stephen approaches millinery with visionary expertise and takes inspiration from everything and everywhere.'
36 Great Queen Street, WC2B 5AA
stephenjonesmillinery.com

3 Wayne Shires

'Wayne has been integral to gay London club life since the late 1980s. His nights include parties at his clubs Sub Station, Crash and, most recently, East Bloc and Bloc Bar. He is continually reinventing the scene and exploring ideas of what club life is all about.'
Bloc Bar: 18 Kentish Town Road, NW1 9NX
East Bloc: 217 City Road, EC1V 1JN;
eastbloc.co.uk

4 Judy Blame

'He's made a career of reinventing mundane objects into things of beauty. Judy Blame is the man who, since starting in the 1980s as a jewellery maker, stylist and artist with a discerning eye, has created a world where he continually questions the way we look at things. He was involved with Christopher Nemeth at the legendary House of Beauty and Culture, styles Neneh Cherry to this day and has collaborated with Kim Jones at Louis Vuitton.'

5 Boy George

'George's well-documented career has had an array of ups and downs, but he's always an inspiration. I met him in the late '70s and never cease to be amazed by his abilities to express himself through not only music but writing and personal style.'
boygeorgeuk.com

Princess Julia onstage at her one-woman show at The Glory, 2015.

Dover Street Market

It was a very exciting moment when Rei Kawakubo brought her boutique to London, and I'm still thrilled every time I visit. Now in its second incarnation at Haymarket, the multi-floor, multi-brand space has expanded threefold into this former Burberry emporium. Depending on your bank balance it tends to be more for browsing than buying (a bridesmaid's budget would only afford me a detachable collar instead of the actual dress!). Comme des Garçons' own designs are scattered among pockets of other collections, which can include anything from Alaïa to post-grad designers in this democratically devised fashionista's wishlist. Each brand has its own distinct visual merchandising, too: a metal dinosaur sculpture winds its way around pillars and columns while Margaret Howell designs hang from her trademark Ercol furniture fittings. IDEA Books have a concession for reading material and Michael Costiff has a wing for his World Archive collection. If you're shopped out by the time you climb to the top floor, Rose Bakery is in residence to provide refreshments. Keep an eye on the staff, as they are most probably students next in line for NewGen nominations.

18–22 Haymarket, SW1Y 4DG
london.doverstreetmarket.com

Craig Green's S/S16 space with collaborative sculpture by David Curtis-Ring.

Memphis lamp at IDEA Books.

Duro Olowu

If you love to get lost in layers of exotic textiles in souks or stuck into the archives of ethnographic museums or antique art monographs at book fairs, Duro Olowu's boutique should be on your map. Furniture is upholstered in Olowu's own optical velvet textiles and the floor is scattered with Moroccan multicolour tuft rugs. Piles of artists' hardback books are stacked up and tribal accessories are encased in old shop cabinets like relics. In between these, his own label's signature silk dresses hang as if Barneys had infiltrated Frieze Masters. It's a look inside a creative mind with the aptitude to combine historical knowledge and related aesthetics from disparate sources in one cosmic place.

14 Masons Yard, St James's, SW1Y 6BU
duroolowu.com

On the occasion I visited, there was a Lynette Yiadom-Boakye portrait and a Hamidou Maiga print on the walls and ceramics by Tommaso Corvi-Mora on the shelves.

Liam Hodges's installation at Machine-A, 2016.

Machine-A

London's most cutting-edge independent contemporary fashion concept store was first opened in 2008 by Stavros Karelis. His emphasis on championing new talent means that graduate designers from that time now comfortably hang on the rails next to established names. That's the mix here at Machine-A: Raf Simons shirts rub shoulders with Nasir Mazhar sweaters and Ashish sequins shimmy next to Cottweiler parachute silk shell-suits. Stylist Anna Trevelyan acts as buyer and walking ambassador for the brand by wearing exactly what is new in store. Some exclusive pieces coincide with Fashion Week, so you can pick up styles fresh from the catwalk. Designers take over the exhibition space at the back for installations, and long-term collaborations with Nick Knight's fashion website SHOWstudio bring about seasonal special projects.

13 Brewer Street, W1F 0RH
machine-a.com

Darkroom

London girls Rhonda and Lulu are great fun, and adept at putting together a visual story to make you want everything in their Darkroom store. It's a mix of fashion and furniture with accessories that could be ornaments and vice versa. Products are neatly arranged on fittings and fixtures designed to confuse this crossover even more.

Owing to a graphics and interior design background, these buyers have an eye for a sharp aesthetic. Inspired by Memphis Art Deco (they're Sottsass-obsessed), tribal patterns and bold, bright colour blocking, they rotate seasons on an invented theme. Alongside their in-house line of soft furnishings and stationery, they source artisanal pieces in similar styles to complete a composition of covetable goods. They hand-painted a chequerboard floor to set off these still-life setups and commission artists to make complementary window installations. It is a very specific taste, but so darn tasteful that it's a perfect place for finding gifts for someone special … and, er, yourself.

Darkroom is located on Lamb's Conduit Street (NOT to be mistaken for Conduit Street), which hosts a row of independent retailers. Make sure you have a snoop around the neighbouring small enterprises.

52 Lamb's Conduit Street, WC1N 3LL
darkroomlondon.com

Lazy Oaf

Illustrator Gemma Shiel started selling silly t-shirts online while studying and has now found herself with an international superbrand. From early on she established the fun label with a shop in Carnaby Street and has never looked back. The flagship space encapsulates the cute and kawaii identity and acts as a showroom for the mostly online shop. The staff are always bubbly, so it's worth going in for a chat to get the lowdown on their latest Looney Tunes collaboration.

Classic pieces include the burger beanie hat and colour block backpack. The apparel range extends to full-on selections of kaleidoscopic patterned garms, with complementary phone cases, nail wraps and temporary tattoos. Their new collection launches are fun, with music provided by the pop stars they are dressing, and reminiscent of kids' birthday parties with goody bags of sweets and treats. I even got a signed sticker by Jim Davis from the unveiling of the Garfield line. Jeez!

2 Ganton Street, W1F 7QL
lazyoaf.com

Stephen Jones Millinery

If you're in town needing an occasion hat for Ascot or a fascinator for a wedding, then Stephen Jones is the classic millinery magician in London.

36 Great Queen Street, WC2B 5AA
stephenjonesmillinery.com

Phonica

While you're losing your mind (and, potentially, wallet) on Berwick Street's record shop row, take a sharp swerve on Noel Street to find Phonica. You'll see a doorway plastered with club night promoters' posters—that's it. It's also the place the listed DJs will stop off when they're in town playing the capital's various venues. It's a social spot and the most friendly, accessible record shop for newbies and novices. Everything is laid out in a very clear and uncluttered display so you can see their recommendations and, ultimately, end up walking out with them, even if you hadn't intended on buying anything. I find it's a bit like the way supermarkets sneakily put sweets at the tills so you accidentally slip some in your basket as you wait. At Phonica the candy is hung on the wall behind the shopkeepers—and, as they find the record for your sleeve, you'll spot something else special.

      The shop has been a pharmacy for vinyl junkies since 2003, when vinyl pressing plant/label The Vinyl Factory asked Simon Rigg to set it up. A decade ago record sales were in decline and the area's shops were closing. Phonica has stood the test of time and is the name dropped by other dealers if they don't have what you're after. If you're planning a pit-stop, turn into the layby of the adjacent Brewer Street car park. Here, The Vinyl Factory have an exhibition space where they showcase the artist collaborations they've been working on or hosting. Previous shows have included Trevor Jackson, Quentin Jones and Richard Mosse.

51 Poland Street, W1F 7LZ
phonicarecords.com

Sounds of the Universe
7 Broadwick Street, W1F 0DA
soundsoftheuniverse.com

Sister Ray
Berwick Street Market, 75 Berwick Street, W1F 8TG
sisterray.co.uk

If Music
12 D'Arblay Street, W1F 8DU
ifmusic.co.uk

Ray's Jazz at Foyles
113–119 Charing Cross Road, WC2H 0EB
foyles.co.uk/rays-jazz-classical-music

Intoxica Records
11 Cecil Court, WC2N 4EZ
intoxica.co.uk

Phonica's window celebrating Jamie XX's album *In Colour.*

Berwick Street

Berwick Street is the epicentre of Soho. It's a portal from the Oxford Street squash to the red lights of (Street) Walker's Court. Although Soho's characteristic and crucial underbelly is slipping away, you can still get a sense of it if you stand still for long enough. Behind the fruit and veg stalls and wheelbarrows of marrows are door markings that read 'Models This Way'. The neon backdrop of Brewer Street has been the heartbeat of so many London nightlife scenes, but the most criminal aspect to me is the council's recent policy of conscious cleansing. Gone are the Sunset Cinema, the Soho Review Bar (Tranny Shack Wednesday nights were a personal fave) and Madame Jojos. Now, the nearest thing you can get to a smooch is a frozen yoghurt from a spectrum-lit ice-cream parlour called SNOG. At least the record shops and fabric suppliers are still in situ to define its distinct daytime draw. Dig the crates of world music at Sounds of the Universe and follow with a takeaway box of world cuisine from the market's stellar street food stalls.

Berwick Street, W1
berwickstreetlondon.co.uk

Monmouth Coffee

When searching for an independent café and looking at their caffeine supplier, you might come across Monmouth Coffee roast. This is the distributors' HQ and the place where the eponymous beans began in 1978. It's a very small place, so arrive early doors to be seated or go straight for their infamous filter coffee to take away. In fact, they almost take offence if you order anything different as the barista ladles water across the paper cone funnels. Don't dare ask for a dairy substitute as the milk is the best bit, coming from the creamiest Jersey cows in Somerset. If you must sweeten to taste, check out the organic whole cane sugar from Costa Rica. It's these details that make this the coffee joint to jot down in your hit list. That, and the brioche. Did I mention the brioche?

27 Monmouth Street, WC2H 9EU
monmouthcoffee.co.uk

Bar Italia

I've suggested Monmouth Coffee as the place to pick up a takeaway, but this is my top tip for a place to stay and sip a white coffee while soaking up the atmos. Soho is under threat of cleansing but this is one steadfast establishment that hasn't been affected by any change over the last six decades. Note the ancient cash register as your order is rung through the clunking system while the barista butters you up with some smooth Italian flattery. They are self-assured enough to boast the finest and friendliest coffee in town, which is their own secret blend. Their Gaggia coffee machine doesn't have a water filter, so no salts are run through it and its temperature is set to less than boiling so the coffee doesn't burn. I just love standing at the Art Deco mirrored counter to sip my espresso and witness the mix of Soho regulars signal for their drinks without explanation. It's open from 7 am until 3 am, so the mix changes with the time as Ronnie Scott's Jazz Club opposite makes it a musical late-night haunt. I also enjoy the guilty pleasure of a side glance at MTV on the telly to see what's new in the world of music videos. Honestly, that's part of the reason I go in. It's a trashy confession but, then again, it's Soho, so it goes with the territory!

22 Frith Street, W1D 4RF
baritaliasoho.co.uk

Indian YMCA

Cheap as chips or, in this case, cheap as chapatis. London residents will be livid that I've lifted the lid on this relatively undocumented curry revelation. The public are allowed to plunder the visitors' canteen for the special set meal deal. Just make sure you arrive on time for the early supper slot, 7 to 8:30 pm.

41 Fitzroy Square, W1T 6AQ
indianymca.org

Diwana Bhel Poori House

Tucked neatly into Drummond Street is a district for the delicacy of tasty pancake pockets known as dosas.

121–123 Drummond Street, NW1 2HL

Langan's Brasserie

I'm not going to lie to you, this is a pricy one—but it's the legacy from its original 1970s patrons that makes it appeal to me. Artists who couldn't afford owner Michael Caine's Parisienne-style café paid in paintings. As a result, the walls of this relaxed Mayfair restaurant read as a gallery, boasting works by the likes of Lucien Freud and Francis Bacon. There are also notable David Hockney portraits of Celia Birtwell and founder Peter Langan illustrating the menu. Read it and weep. Literally. Tears of joy.

Stratton Street, W1J 8LB
langansbrasserie.com

The French House

You're bang in the heart of Theatreland but don't want to be ripped off or waste time in a tourist hellhole. Find Dean Street and The French House is the answer to your prayers, in the form of a perfect thespian watering hole. Beer is only served in small measures so you can dip in and out. In the summer, take a bottle of cloudy Breton *cidre* outside onto the street and soak up Soho's infectious energy—it's a totally democratic demographic of drinkers. You can see evidence of the bar's spectacular heritage framed on the walls and look around the room to spot the old-timer Beat poet regulars. With a menu of 30 champagnes and wines by the glass, there's good reason to return to work your way through the list.

49 Dean Street, W1D 5BG
frenchhousesoho.com

Phoenix Artist Club
1 Phoenix Street/Charing Cross Road, WC2H 8BU
phoenixartistclub.com

The New Evaristo Club (Trisha's)
57 Greek St, W1D 3DX

Top 5 Cocktail Haunts

David Piper

As Global Ambassador for Hendrick's Gin, David Piper is either discovering botanicals in far-flung rainforests or delivering rose and cucumber concoctions to uncharted territories. His homework legitimately involves working his way through cocktail menus until lock-ins: a vocation that doubles as a vacation. This dandy earned his stripes by sampling the delights of the world's bars before his dream job was specially tailored for him. Here we have lounge-lizard liquor tips from a high-proof source.

1 Happiness Forgets

'I wish I lived close, but, then again, I'd end up in there far too often. The smallest and cosiest and neighbourhoodiest, it's heartwarming and comfortable and delicious and free-spirited and it makes time slow down. A lot.'
8–9 Hoxton Square, N1 6NU
happinessforgets.com

2 DUKES Bar

'I'm madly in love with the dry gin martini —I will launch into raptures about its magic powers given half a sip. They will almost certainly make you other drinks there if you ask, but go for the martinis, it's a special experience. Probably not more than two. If you go in the afternoon and manage to escape again while it's still light, golly! You might have hit some sort of jackpot!'
35 St James's Place, SW1A 1NY
dukeshotel.com/dukes-bar

3 Experimental Cocktail Club Chinatown

'The original Experimental Cocktail Club in Paris was the bar that first reawakened my deep love for sitting in a beautiful little bar drinking strong, cold concoctions full of subtle flavour, and I've spent so much time in all of their places that they feel like second homes. Having this in London is a deep link to some of the most brilliant aspects of my time in France, and life in general.'
13a Gerrard Street, W1D 5PS
chinatownecc.com

4 Artesian at The Langham

'Fun—fun that effortlessly and often very sillily transcends what would, in anyone else's hands, be a rather constrained "luxury" offering. Wonderful hospitality, and more madness than any other bar in town.'
1C Portland Place, W1B 1JA
artesian-bar.co.uk

5 American Bar at the Savoy

'Classic. Probably nowhere else in the world captures that "idea" of cocktails, the elegance and glamour and beauty, as well. They revived the bar's tradition as one of the cradles of cocktail culture by using a time machine not to take us back to the past, but to bring a little of the Deco era— the true essence I mean, not just design cues, gorgeous as they are—and shake and strain it into reality in the modern day. So many bars want to be, look, feel old-fashioned these days, but the Savoy has the heritage, the skills, the team and the budget to do it without it feeling like they've even tried. Sitting there makes you feel special.'
The Savoy, Strand, WC2R 0EU
fairmont.com/savoy-london/dining/americanbar

David at Artesian, Portland Place.

Experimental Cocktail Club Chinatown

I'm always a bit sceptical of someone making me a cocktail. I see it as both a science and an art form so tend to opt out rather than risk something that seems as though it's been washed up on the rocks. However, I will happily be led astray into the ECC and put my fate into the hands of these mixologist masters. Either choose from the menu or throw out some abstract nouns and they will devise a new recipe in reply. It's up a flight of stairs behind an unmarked door in Chinatown, so be prepared to be as glamorous as Jack Nicholson and Faye Dunaway to get past the disgruntled doorman.

13a Gerrard Street, W1D 5PS
chinatownecc.com

Trader Vic's Tiki Bar

This is the most incongruous and inexplicable example of planning in the history of London's high-end hospitality. In the basement of the Hilton hotel lies Trader Vic's Tiki Bar—Home of the Original Mai Tai®. And my oh my, you'll have an almighty great night here, not just because of their kitsch, boat-size drinking vessels, but because of the volume of liquor they hold. The decor is like something out of Elvis Presley's *Blue Hawaii* movie, with a bamboo hut bar, totem pole woodwork and taxidermy turtles flying mid-air. This exotic destination is a little remote, located out on the Pacific Park Lane, but well worth the voyage as it's so truly unique. There's only so much 'on-trend' hype I can take and this fantasy cocktail haven is the perfect, unrivalled, reliable antidote.

22 Park Lane, W1K 1BE
tradervicslondon.com

25

Great Portland Street

Regent's Park

2(

13

2

Oxford Circus

7

Green Park

22

17

14

41

Euston

9

Euston Square

Russell Square

33

Goodge Street

1

39

Holborn

Tottenham
Court Road

24

40

38

16

32

12

6

15

30

29

Covent Garden

31

11

37

10

Leicester Square

23

18

Temple

21

8

27

34

5

4

Charing Cross

Embankment

3

Koko

It's called Koko—it says so in massive lit letters on the front. But most Londoners still refer to it as Camden Palace, its precursor, which was started by the singer Steve Strange in the 1980s. Since the New Romantic era and more recent rundown indie nights, it's had an extensive restoration and face lift. Tim Walker shot Vivienne Westwood's portrait here and fashion brands have held launch nights at the venue. A standout memory for me was Agyness Deyn hosting her Burberry perfume party with an outsize chandelier made out of scent bottle components and the entrance boxed in by false mirror walls. It was one of those nights where corporate execs sipped champagne next to drag queens throwing up tinsel. The balcony on the front of the building is a unique smoking terrace with a fantastic view out onto Camden High Street for people-watching, as well as a stunning sunset trap in the summer and quiet spot to catch up for a natter in between bands. The height of the building is split up into many tiered balconies, which are great fun to run around on and find hidden enclaves and vantage points. It's not a venue to stay still in for too long because there's so much to uncover.

1a Camden High Street, NW1 7JE
koko.uk.com

Gilles Peterson's Worldwide Awards at Koko, 2016.

The Forum

For a decade my local live music venue has been the Forum (now the O2 Forum Kentish Town), so it holds a special place in my heart. This affection dates back to the 14-year-old me witnessing the Leigh Bowery-fronted band Minty as the support act to Pulp, and the magic of a naked Nicola Bateman dressed in a transparent shower-curtain frame with flashing fairy light trim. I've had subsequent religious experiences here over the years, from Peaches appearing from the side box to begin her *Impeach My Bush* record tour to Bobby Womack's comeback with *The Bravest Man in the Universe*. I've been grateful for the stroll home after epic hours of dancing both at a Theo Parrish 'Footwork' performance and a funk fest with the original P-Funk legend George Clinton.

     I have a little game with myself where I guess the band playing on any particular night after looking at the demographic of the audience emerging from the Underground. The Forum is a mid-sized venue so always has a busy schedule, with bands that might have booked it before their breakthrough album release and subsequent exploded fan base. Next door to the historic Bull & Last pub, it's traditionally been a destination for discovering new music. Remember to look up, as this former Art Deco cinema has a beautiful ceiling.

9–17 Highgate Road, NW5 1JY
theforumlondon.com

The Roundhouse

The majority of London's large live music venues are former theatres, cinemas and dancehalls. They have a decaying charm but share a similar sound quality and atmosphere. One building that blows the roof off that formula is the quite literally round Roundhouse. Nowadays, it's an international performing arts venue plus creative space for young people. However, the circular turntable at its centre was built for rotating and repairing train engines in the 1850s. After twenty years, technological advancement rendered it redundant, and the building went on to house various cutting-edge arts centres. The 1960s saw Pink Floyd, Jimi Hendrix, Fleetwood Mac and The Doors play here. In the 1970s it turned theatrical, hosting Andy Warhol's play *Pork* and dancer Lindsay Kemp's productions. Punk was also prevalent, with shows from Patti Smith, The Ramones, The Sex Pistols and Blondie. In the 1980s, dance choreographers held residencies here, with the Michael Clark Company and De La Guarda making full use of the open space, flying around on stunt wires.

In 2006 the National Lottery contributed to a £30 million redevelopment scheme and the resultant new build is architecturally praised. Large-scale installations are now part of the programme, and in 2009 David Byrne even turned the structure into a musical instrument. As a visitor you could personally 'Play the Building' by sitting at a pump organ linked up to motors and compressors with hammers on the Victorian metal pillars—a sound installation that was so site-specific that the site itself was the medium.

Chalk Farm Road, NW1 8EH
roundhouse.org.uk

Performance artist Scottee at The Roundhouse.

Ivon Hitchens's mural at Cecil Sharp House.

Cecil Sharp House

Built on a triangular plot of land in 1929, this hall was placed in the apex at the back to protect neighbours from noise. At a time before amplification you've got to wonder what kind of ceilidhs were kicking off at the English Folk Dance and Song Society. Set up in memory of revivalist Cecil Sharp, the society is devoted to restoring the heritage of country folk arts, music and moves, which continues today with concerts, dances and workshops. That includes morris dance classes, barn dancing and ukulele jams. I've included it in my guide to London because it's an underdog in the city's gig circuit. Acoustic musicians like Laura Marling and Mumford & Sons tread the boards here before they hit the big time and win Brit Awards.

If you're in the area for a walk on Primrose Hill, make another visit in the daylight. Ivon Hitchens's 69-foot-long mural in the main hall is a glorious symphony of colour, rhythms and dance—what he called 'eye-music'. The 1950s abstract work uses a palette that makes the most of the natural light, from cooler shades of blue and green on the sunnier west side to warmer tones on the east.

2 Regent's Park Road, NW1 7AY
cecilsharphouse.org

Scala
275 Pentonville Road, N1 9NL
scala.co.uk

The Boogaloo
312 Archway Road, N6 5AT
theboogaloo.co.uk

Alan's Records

I'm a latecomer to the 21-year success of the Aladdin's cave that is Alan's Records.
That's because it's at the very top of the Northern Line in East Finchley. It wasn't until
my uncle pointed it out to me while driving home for Christmas once that I was alerted
to this treasure chest. On my first trip, I picked up a half 'n' half coffee at the café
nearby, and there was DJ and producer Mr Thing and a crew of music heads, also
about to head over to Alan's. Before I'd even crossed the threshold my fingers were
wriggling with digger's twitch. The customers are a clear indication of the crossover
of every genre stocked here. There's something for everyone and a lot of it is offered
at affordable prices. Alan is literally on the tools and happy to help you listen to your
overloaded arms' worth of selections. He's even got a key-cutting service—so you
can't cut the guy down for diversifying! If you're driving up in anticipation of a large
haul, look up local free parking to dodge the inspector lurking on the meters directly
outside. The best date for your diary is the first week of the new year, when he clears
the collection with a half-price sale on everything.

218 High Road, N2 9AY
alansrecords.com

AudioGold
308–310 Park Road, N8 8LA
audiogold.co.uk/record-shop

All Ages Records
27 Pratt Street, NW1 0BG
allagesrecords.com

Lucky Seven
127 Stoke Newington Church Street, N16 0UH

Out on the Floor
10 Inverness Street, NW1 7HJ

Zen Records
69 Broad Lane, N15 4DJ

Black Cotton
Unit 456 Camden Market

Record Detective Agency
492 Green Lanes, N13 5PA

Sounds that Swing
88 Parkway, NW1 7AN
nohitrecords.co.uk

Electric Knife Records
16b Fortess Road, NW5 2EU
electrickniferecords.co.uk

Second-hand records, tapes and books at Lucky Seven.

Alan's Records, East Finchley.

Dividers with hand-drawn type at Out on the Floor.

Flashback Records

If I'm reviewing record shops by the staff that stock the bins, this is how it would go: Music & Goods Exchange guys are the moles of the business, with half-shut eyes from never emerging from the 10 hour shifts in the dark and hyper-mobile hands from shovelling stacks of 7"s. Flashback, on the other hand, is the flashier side of the second-hand record shop dealership. I get a feeling these guys are running their own record labels from under the counter as opposed to running out of Rich Tea in the biscuit tin under there. This is the more self-conscious set-up for new-school selectors. It's a mix of both the latest releases and vintage vinyl, so it's a one-stop shop for a pre-meditated purchase and spontaneous dig. The formula has found such great success from its first shop in Highbury in 1997 that it now has three sites between Crouch End and Shoreditch.

50 Essex Road, N1 8LR
flashback.co.uk

The Screen on the Green

The Screen on the Green stands out proud with its neon-lit semicircle facade bearing the title of the week's feature show. It's got a sentimental, old-school, Saturday night at the movies vibe. With a bar installed in the main auditorium and two-seater sofas with footrests, this is the place to park yourself for a weekend double-feature show. It's an Everyman premium venue, but the ticket price is well worth it for the arthouse premieres. In the past I have attended UK exclusive director's panel-discussion unveilings of *The September Issue* and Bruce Weber's *Let's Get Lost*, after which the photographer stayed behind for signings and to say hello. According to Bruce, the film's star, the legendary late jazz musician Chet Baker, would have loved this cinema, so there's a soulful rating worth noting!

83 Upper Street, N1 0NP
everymancinema.com

The Zabludowicz Collection

London is so big that tourists and residents alike can easily miss what's going on. For me, that undetected pot of gold came in the form of a gallery called the Zabludowicz Collection. Directly north of town, between Camden and Kentish Town, is this Corinthian-style converted Methodist church that is now a Mecca for modern art. The gallery has its own extensive collection (both here and in New York) with which it opened in 2007. New shows are commissioned from artists linked to the collection, such as Ryan Trecartin and Lizzie Fitch.

176 Prince of Wales Road, NW5 3PT
zabludowiczcollection.com/london

A Guyton/Walker piece in the 'Zabludowicz Collection: 20 Years' exhibition, 2015.

Camden Market

The Britpop-obsessed teenage me would spend Saturdays at Portobello Road and Sundays at Camden. The railway arches of the Stables Market here are a labyrinth of original Levi's, 1960s psychedelic dresses, '70s ska suits and '80s casual sportswear. Now packed with parkas, the stables were originally built as a hospital for horses, which were used to pull barges along the canal. The market took over as the waterway haulage ceased trade in the 1970s, and Sundays became popular at a time when the law still forbade shops opening on the holy day of rest. Despite the Sunday Trading Act of 1994 having turned town into a retail therapy theme park, Camden has never lost its appeal.

     The bridge still serves as a base for punks to pose for photos and point you in the direction of the tattoo and piercing parlours. Shop fronts are decorated with oversize signage, continuing that very British folk tradition, as celebrated in the artist Jeremy Deller's anthropological projects. Inside are shelves of tacky toot and counterfeit fashion, which I'd give a wide berth to. The same goes for the congealed noodles in the food court. The only consumable I would condone in Camden comes from the fresh-pressed orange juice carts and, at a push, potentially the doughnut stands if you're about to pass out from partying the night before.

     I'm a Camden resident and, for all its icky naff nonsense, I still hold it close to my heart. I'll never forget the mornings of seeing Amy Winehouse's beehive bobbing about or forget the roses laid at her house when she bowed out. You can still see street art in her memory and some of the city's best graffiti on the residential roads. Camden is a definite destination for the to-do list; just make sure you have a quick escape route planned. Either cross the bridge to Primrose Hill or ascend Haverstock Hill for Hampstead Heath.

Camden High Street, NW1 8NH
camdenmarket.com

Camden Town bridge mural.

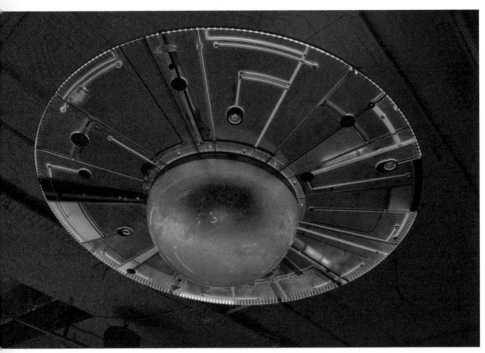

Camden Market has overcome a couple of major fires, but fluoro hyperreal kawaii clubwear store Cyberdog is still biting on like a bionic canine phoenix.

A spectrum of visors.

Ska memorabilia.

Walden Books

Before I started stashing spare cash for crate-digging, I used to save my pocket money for Walden Books. Essentially, I switched my investments from hardbacks to hard wax; my dad is convinced both are giving my house subsidence. Walden's is a walk across the road from Camden Market and a beautiful vision, dripping in wisteria, in the summer. It has an ever-replenished selection of second-hand, rare and out of print art (and some literature) books. My favourite section is the fashion photography shelf, with titles you neglected to collect first time round and ancient treats you've never seen before. I've found so many Cecil Beaton wonders that I've had to start snapping them up for other people too.

38 Harmood Street, NW1 8DP
waldenbooks.co.uk

Keats House Museum, Gardens & Library

Broaden your vocab and inspire a spark in your literary flow at the home of 'bright star' John Keats. The poet spent time in this Regency villa writing words to his forbidden love, who lived next door. See his life's work in letters, photographs, manuscripts and even engagement rings in the very place where his life's story unfolded. It's absolutely incredible that, in such a short life, Keats left a monumental international legacy without ever realising his own importance. That is why I think this is such a special place to discover and honour one of the city's most significant historical talents. It also plays the vital role of running a community library in the grounds, which is 100 per cent self-funded and run by volunteers. With over 20,000 items available to borrow and a full programme of poetry readings, talks, walks, tours, workshops, special displays and family days, it's a lush London address for your little black book.

10 Keats Grove, NW3 2RR
keatscommunitylibrary.org.uk

Reconstructions of Keats's life.

Top 5 Food Spots

Mark Ogus

To help you pick(le) your way through London's minefield of food offerings, I've asked a man who knows a thing or two about how much love goes into cooking. Mark Ogus takes so much care over curing meats that he spends the whole week preparing pastrami and salt beef for his Saturday stall. His Jewish soul food emporium Monty's Deli is named after his grandfather, and the beef brisket is soaked from scratch to the family's secret recipe. It's sliced up, piled on rye with Russian dressing, sauerkraut and Swiss cheese, then toasted and served with a pickle on the side. That's a Reuben, and this former Vincent Vincent and the Villains frontman is famed for the very best pastrami in the city.

1 The Water Margin

'My Chinese restaurant of choice since I was a little boy! If the world was about to end, I'd want to go out eating their char siu pork, roast duck and rice and a portion of choy sum in oyster sauce on the side.'
96 Golders Green Road, NW11 8HB

2 Song Que

'This place is the perfect hangover refuge, despite its pistachio green interior. I've spent many a Sunday lunchtime here slowly coming back to life over a fresh and fragrant pho soup.'
134 Kingsland Road, E2 8DY
songque.co.uk

3 Patty & Bun

'Burgers are everywhere now. Londoners can look to their left and right at any time and see burgers. However, I don't get tired of Patty & Bun burgers because they are delicious. 'Nuff said.'
22/23 Liverpool Street, EC2M 7PD
pattyandbun.co.uk

4 Mangal 1 Ocakbasi

'Kebabs at Mangal are magnificent: meats charred to perfection on the open-faced grill by a sweaty expert who knows just when I'm ready. The salads are also great, with crunchy mooli, pickled peppers, fresh rocket and thinly sliced onions sprinkled with sumac, dressed only with lemon juice. Mouth-watering.'
10 Arcola Street, E8 2DJ
mangal1.com

5 Silk Road

'If you live in London and haven't been to Silk Road, then you're wasting your time. This is Szechuan food of the highest order, with hand-pulled noodles freshly made in-house, deep flavoursome spiced broths and the most incredible tasting wok-fried cabbage (the dish is called home-style cabbage), to name just a few of the delights on offer here. Plus, it's cheap!'
49 Camberwell Church Street, SE5 8TR

Mark at his restaurant, Monty's Deli.

Yeni Umut 2000 Ocakbasi

Dalston is London's destination for Turkish mangal (barbeque), and there are a few names of note when investigating the nominations. The people's winner, which boasts a 'Simply the Best' slogan t-shirt (merch for sale on request!), is Mangal 1 Ocakbasi on Arcola Street. I beg to differ, and side step off the main drag to Yeni Umut on Crossway. This has a mad amount of dips in its mezze to start and poussin to mix up its mixed grill.

6 Crossway, N16 8HX

Mangal 2

If you want a tourist experience head to Mangal 2, famed for its devout regulars, artist duo Gilbert & George, who routinely walk from Spitalfields to eat there every night. I like to see them to check in on the seasons changing according to their attire—fur deerstalker hats for winter and light tweed suits for spring.

4 Stoke Newington Road, N16 8BH
mangal2.com

El Rincon Quiteno

I tend to err on the veggie side of the spectrum, but El Rincon Quiteno is unapologetically meat on meat. In fact, more precisely, it's a fried egg on meat, on refried beans. The traditional Ecuadorian/Bolivian restaurant is a family affair and a humble home-style establishment, with equally humble pricing.

235 Holloway Road, N7 8HG

St John's Tavern

If you're visiting the UK on a Sunday you HAVE to try a roast dinner here.
It's the Holy Grail of traditional English cuisine.

91 Junction Rd, N19 5QU
stjohnstavern.com

Melrose and Morgan

Melrose and Morgan's initials spell MM, and that 'MMMMMMMMMMMMM — YUM'
would be solely for its Chelsea bun. I walk along the canal in Camden to exit at
Primrose Hill, turning to pop up right under the awning of this spot. That's exactly
where I like to sit to enjoy a coffee. It's a grocer's and deli/café that puts out freshly
prepared seasonal dishes from the onsite kitchen using ingredients grown and
reared in the UK. If the Chelsea buns have sold out, it's never a chore to sink your
teeth into any of the other delicacies on the counter here. It's low-key and it's quality.
Just the way I like it.

42 Gloucester Avenue, NW1 8JD
melroseandmorgan.com

Camden Town Brewery Bar

You'll notice Camden Town Brewery taps in pubs across the city, and it's here that you'll be sampling the brews onsite, exactly where they are fermented and filtered. Every single beer is on pump at the bar and you can even book a tour to have a snoop around the coppers beforehand. Weekends are catered by a calendar of pop-up street food vendors, so you can have Japanese soboro on Saturday or jerk chicken on Sunday, all swilled down with a Strawberry Hells Forever. The outdoor cobbled street is a perfect hidden hangout on a bustling warm summer's night.

55–59 Wilkin Street Mews, NW5 3NN
camdentownbrewery.com/brewery-bar

The Good Mixer

Pool players are an unexpected victim of space becoming such a valuable commodity in London—who knew? It seems that pubs would rather pack out their poky floors with drinkers sinking pints rather than pinks. Apart from dedicated pool halls like Efes in Dalston or Canavan's in Peckham, there aren't many options. Apart from the exceptional Good Mixer pub in Camden, that is, which has two tables so there's always a chance to get your pound down for the next play. On Monday nights, the winner stays on in the weekly tournament. Notably and notoriously, it was also the definitive venue of the birth of Britpop, with Blur propping up the bar and, more recently, Amy Winehouse making selections on the juke box.

30 Inverness Street, NW1 7HJ
thegoodmixer.com

The dog crèche at Parliament Hill.

Parliament Hill

To get some perspective and a tingle up your spine, climb to the summit of Parliament Hill for something spectacular. This is my personal favourite spot for a panoramic view of London because it's possible to come at an off-peak time and have a very quiet and personal moment. There's a bench on which to perch and look out across the whole epic skyline for a bird's eye view of the city's sights. Nothing else offers quite the same sense of peace as realising your own small part in the scheme of things and how beautiful London is over the whole sum of its parts. It's no surprise that many films have used this plot for its poetic position, but the best thing is that it can be yours and yours only for a moment of mindful magic without distraction.

Parliament Hill Lido
Hampstead Heath, NW5 1NA

Parliament Hill Athletics Track
Parliament Hill Fields, Highgate Road, NW5 1QR

Primrose Hill

If Parliament Hill is just too far north to go for a scenic view of London, then Primrose Hill provides a beautiful second best. Exit Regent's Park and cross the canal to climb the incline and recline on the benches at the top to see across the spectrum of skyscrapers. Primrose Hill Panorama is so precious that it's a protected viewpoint of London.

Primrose Hill Road, NW3 3NA

The view from the summit at Parliament Hill Fields.

Chapel Market

The weekend farmer's market harks back to the original one held at this location, which was the first in London. On Sundays, this specialist space has seasonal flowers, organic veg and free-range meat. If you want an authentic taste of the area, nip into Manzes Pie & Mash. There's no more traditional East End dish than a helping of eel, chilli vinegar and liquor.

Between Liverpool Road and Baron Street, N1 9EX

Parliament Hill Farmer's Market

If you want to differentiate farmers' markets by their distinct features, Parliament Hill Fields is the one with the view. On your way up to the panoramic shot of the city from the pinnacle of Hampstead Heath, you should get your take-away coffee from here. There's a dog crèche at the gate where you can leave your pooch while you peruse the produce. Held in a school playground, it's a typically North London affair, with only the finest of foods and no filler: rare breed meat, game in season, buffalo mozzarella, biodynamic eggs, artisanal bread, raw milk, fish stalls with oysters opened ready to eat and barbequed venison burgers.

William Ellis School, Highgate Road, NW5 1RN
lfm.org.uk/markets/parliament-hill

Rowans Tenpin Bowl

That Slush Puppy cracked-out excitement of a childhood birthday party outing to the local sports centre whooshes straight back at Rowans Tenpin Bowl. You've got to get past the games arcade, pool room and ping pong tables to hit the 24-lane bowling alley. If that's not enough options for you, there are giant screens projecting football matches for the gents and karaoke for the ladies. Lace up in the appropriate footwear and start quoting *The Big Lebowski* as you go for a full strike (or straight down the gutter, depending on how long it's been since you last went!). Now the Trocadero is a no-go, this is the spot for a virtual Super Mario spin and tournament of 'ting, ting, ting' Space Hockey.

10 Stroud Green Road, N4 2DF
rowans.co.uk

Alexandra Palace

Although it's named Alexandra Palace (or Ally Pally) now, it was originally called the People's Palace. In 1873 it was opened as a public centre of recreation, education and entertainment. To this day it's a destination for concerts, exhibitions, ice skating and, most importantly, its epic Palm Court Victorian conservatory. However, the surrounding park is also an attraction, from the boating lake to landscaped gardens, woodland and open grassland. There's plenty to occupy school escapees too, with a skate park, pitch and putt, soft-play adventure playground and deer park. The main date to get in your diary is the annual Guy Fawkes firework celebrations in the first week of November. This is when Ally Pally's own panoramic London viewpoint is painted with floral explosions of gunpowder. (Ironically, the bomb squad were called on the day I visited to snap this photo because security found my unattended camera bag and were on high alert for the World Darts Championship! London, calm down.)

Alexandra Palace Way, N22 7AY
alexandrapalace.com

Kenwood Ladies' Pond

Although London is my home and I love it, I'm constantly preoccupied by an ambition to see the rest of the world—except when I'm swimming here. It's like my own private oasis because I go on my own and people don't know about it. I cycle there very early in the morning or last thing at night just before it closes, when it's empty. There are beautiful flowers in the long grass and green parakeets (and a kingfisher too, if you're lucky) in the trees. There's nowhere else quite like it. The community of hardcore regulars features older ladies in sparkly turbans; I love listening in to their small talk. It's open all year so if you are brave, break the ice and join the annual Christmas Day outing.

Hampstead Heath, NW5 1QR
klpa.org.uk

Top 5 Running Tips

Charlie Dark

'Charlie Dark Changed My Life' has become a slogan on some of the race t-shirts and banners of his running crew. Despite his name, he brings light into the room wherever his striking foot falls. A spearhead figure in the urban running Bridge the Gap movement representing the UK, he's a spokesman on the subject. The musician and poet imparts words of wisdom like Aslan, exhaling healing magic with each breath. I can't believe he is there loyally every week, without exception. Running the London Marathon with his guidance was one of the best days of my life. I hope that one time we run to Buckingham Palace, we're there to cheer him getting a medal from Her Majesty—because this man deserves an MBE. I asked Charlie for his rules for running success.

1 Running Sucks

'Running sucks when you first start. It's hard and progress can be slow. Don't think of it as running, but learning to move through your city in a new way. Turn your city into a game board and see what areas you can mark off by reaching them on foot. Keep the early adventures short and reward yourself for small victories. The early days are the best running days so enjoy every step and remember to smile.'

2 Make Every Run Epic

'Find epic places to run—places that inspire you—and pair those runs with a kicking soundtrack to help you along the way. Make every run an adventure through your city and seek out the new. These are the moments to draw upon when the running gets tough, especially on race day.'

3 Record, Document, Nerd Out

'Remember when you were a kid and your teacher set you a project and you geeked out and really went to town on the research and presentation—and then you got a bad mark and never did it again? Well, this is a chance to redeem yourself and get your revenge. A 5k/10k/marathon plan is 10 to 16 weeks of your life. Get that scrapbook out, take progress pics and record the transformation as you turn into a better version of you.

Make a wall chart and put it somewhere you can't escape it; cross off the progress with a big red pen. Take care of your training and your training will take care of you.'

4 Dress Like an Athlete, Think Like an Athlete

'Even when you are sweating it's okay to look good, so treat yourself to some kit that makes you feel good and take that running swagger to the road. You might be dying inside, but at least you look like a million dollars.'

5 It's Not How Fast You Go, it's How You Cross the Finish Line

'Think length of time you can run for, not distance you can run, and watch the miles swiftly roll by. Learn to run with feeling and, if need be, take off your watch and concentrate on how running makes you feel. If you can learn to run with a smile on your face, you can run farther than you could ever imagine. Cross the finish line like a boss and consider it a job well done. Two hours or four hours, the distance remains the same.'

Charlie at home, against a Naomi Edmonson mural that is part of her *Survival Techniques* series.

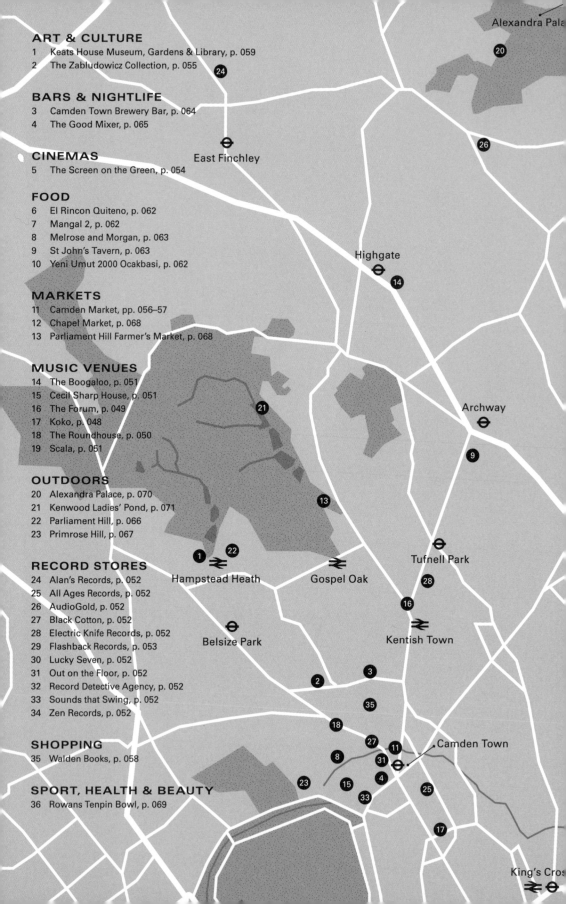

Alexandra Pala

East Finchley

Highgate

Archway

Tufnell Park

Hampstead Heath

Gospel Oak

Kentish Town

Belsize Park

Camden Town

King's Cros

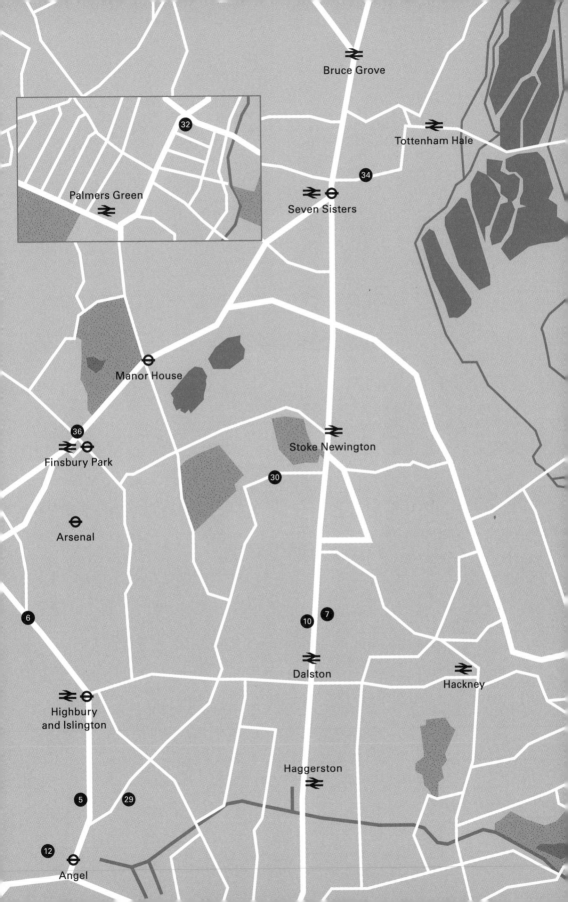

London Fields Lido

It's not by any means the longest pool in London, but it's definitely the most patronised in alternative lifestyle haven London Fields. In summer it's the place to sunbathe and be seen in your smalls. In winter it's a destination for sporty folk such as my studio mate, who attends every morning without fail, come rain, shine or snow. There's even been a book published of photographic portraits of these peculiar all-weather resistance swimmers in the rising steam. Apparently it's all about wearing flip-flops to traverse the ice and getting straight into a hot shower before lowering yourself into the tepid depths.

London Fields West Side, E8 3EU
better.org.uk/leisure/london-fields-lido

Marawa's Hula School/Majorettes

Marawa's the Amazing's outdoor group hula classes set to a dancehall soundtrack are the most fun experience of exercise I've ever had. My abs aching afterwards aren't an issue; it's more the muscles in my cheeks hurting from laughing continuously for an hour. When she is away on her travels she has a troupe, The Majorettes, who take over the reins (and hoops) on her behalf. Check out where and when they will be spinning next on her site.

marawatheamazing.com

London Aquatics Centre

We were incredibly lucky to get the Olympics in London in 2012 and be left with world-leading sports facilities. Legendary British architect Zaha Hadid's pool is one of the best for swimmers of all abilities. It's bloody massive, beautiful and great fun. There aren't just swimming lanes and lessons but diving and even paddleboard coaching, which I've attended. For the longest uninterrupted lengths in London, head to the London Aquatics Centre at Stratford.

Queen Elizabeth Olympic Park, E20 2ZQ
londonaquaticscentre.org

Stretch Yoga

If you're a yoga bunny—or buck—Stretch Yoga is the retreat for you. Founder Carl Faure started Boys of Yoga to open it up to fella-friendly sessions.

6 Ada Street, E8 4QU
59 Columbia Rd, E2 7RG
stretchlondon.org
boysofyoga.com

Calli Popham, instructor at Stretch Yoga.

Epping Forest

The most easterly of London's parks and the most ancient. The woodland
is internationally renowned for its pollarded oak, beech and hornbeam trees.

Victoria Park
Grove Road, E3 5TB

Barbican Conservatory

The Hanging Gardens of Barbican are like a mini Kew Gardens located next
to the art gallery exhibition hall. It's the second largest conservatory in London after
the one at Kew, but this urban jungle is just as exciting. You can be transplanted into
somewhere totally tropical in town. Terrapins peek out of the rock pools in the shade
of palms. Succulents and cacti prickle on the mezzanine level while birdsong cascades
from the aviary. Only open to the public on Sundays, it's a popular spot for wedding
parties. Keep your eye on the Barbican's events listings as some activities are billed
inside this temperate house, such as the Bauhaus costume party I threw there in 2012.

Silk Street, EC2Y 8DS
barbican.org.uk/visitor-information/conservatory

My visit to Urs Fischer's *Honeymoon Suite* installation, part of Doug Aitken's 'Station to Station: 30-Day Happening' programme of events, 2015.

Barbican

When I was a kid my mum likened a trip to the Barbican to Dorothy following the Yellow Brick Road to Oz, owing to the yellow line painted along the floor of the complex to help visitors navigate its maze of Brutalist buildings. Despite years of attending events here I still get lost, but as the site also offers amenities like a gym, shop and launderette for the residents, there could be worse places to be stuck!

This utopian dream took over a decade to build. The architecture of the various apartment blocks, ponds and fountains is a perfect backdrop for a romantic and cultured coffee date. Step inside and you can get lost looking at the koi carp in the tropical conservatory, or catch a free art show in the Curve gallery. Come back at night and Europe's largest multi-purpose arts venue contains concert halls, theatre auditoriums, cinemas and late gallery opening events. It's home to the London Symphony Orchestra, the Michael Clark Dance Company and, previously, the Royal Shakespeare Company, who still show in their former residence. My favourite aspect of the Barbican is the attention to detail in the installation of their main exhibitions. I happen to think it's the best arts venue in London.

To fully appreciate the beauty of the Brutalist development, see if you can find a resident to show you inside and unlock the private gardens. Failing that (let's be realistic), come in September during Open House weekend.

Silk Street, EC2Y 8DS
barbican.org.uk

William Morris Gallery

This Georgian house in Walthamstow was once the family home of the teenage William Morris and now acts as the only public gallery devoted to his legacy. The life's work of the designer, craftsman, writer, socialist and campaigner from the Arts and Crafts movement reopened after major redevelopment in 2012. A permanent exhibition and learning centre has been designed to communicate his influence to the largest possible audience. This also includes a temporary space that has so far shown work by Jeremy Deller, Yinka Shonibare and Bob and Roberta Smith. Special events include late-night openings with the artists in residence and a summer festival garden party.

Lloyd Park House, 531 Forest Road, E17 5EH
wmgallery.org.uk

A Yinka Shonibare piece at William Morris Gallery.

V&A Museum of Childhood

I have a theory that fashion, design and style move in a cyclical pattern according to what each generation grew up with. Whatever visual stimulus was present at the time of an artist's formative years has a reactionary impact on their vision, taste and aesthetic. For example, I'm sure growing up in the 1980s has governed my bright, pop, playful approach. All of this can be put to the test and rediscovered at the Museum of Childhood. No matter what era you first began crawling in, you are sure to get a blast from the past in here. On your first visit you move from cabinet to cabinet involuntarily pointing at things you'd totally forgotten: 'Oh my God, I used to have that!' Toys, childhood equipment, costumes, dolls' houses, optical dioramas, puppets, action figures, teddy bears and board games are all organised and arranged in a dream nostalgia trip.

Cambridge Heath Road, E2 9PA
vam.ac.uk

KK Outlet

Once upon a time in the 1990s, the YBAs transformed East London from barren and bleak to buzzworthy. At the height of this takeover, the heart of the action was Hoxton Square, which housed artists' studios, the White Cube Gallery and the Blue Note nightclub. Regeneration and rising rents have since seen artists being outpriced and steadily moving further east. However, Hoxton still holds onto its creative heritage and, while White Cube has moved south, a gallery still remains on the park. KK Outlet is the front-of-house for Dutch communications agency KesselsKramer. The exhibition space and bookshop holds solo shows and group projects that open on First Thursdays—on this day each month, galleries across the area align to host private views so visitors can pop in and out of them all in one trip. The opportunity for art students to pick up a free beer at each, like a game of Pub Golf, comes as a bonus.

42 Hoxton Square, N1 6PB
kkoutlet.com

Top 5 Alternative Workout Spots

Marawa the Amazing

Marawa the Amazing is the jet-setting cabaret act putting a spin on the industry, setting off a tornado of smoke bombs in her trail. Since performing at fashion parties for Jonathan Saunders and Kenzo, she has popped up as a finalist on both *Arabs Got Talent* and *Britain's Got Talent*. She's a hula-hoop world-record breaker and heartbreaker in her Busby Berkeley-inspired tropical bootylicious costumes. The secret to her abs-olutely amazing rope swinging success is a strong core, and here she shines a spotlight on some other show-stopping sports.

1 Royal Festival Hall

'There is a rad dance rehearsal scene at Royal Festival Hall—it's weird. It's like a public space and, most nights, there are dance crews of all types training there. B-boys, salsa dancers, cheerleaders—get in early if you need space!'
Southbank Centre, Belvedere Road, SE1 8XX
southbankcentre.co.uk/venues/royal-festival-hall

2 Gillett Square

'In summer this place becomes home to all our hoop classes and skate classes. We have been working with the council to timetable classes for kids, adults and beginners, so if you want to learn to skate or hoop—this is the spot! If the weather is good it's the best place to be because there is so much room.'
Gillett Place, N16 8JH
gillettsquare.org.uk

3 Water Workout

'Most entertaining workout ever. The disco diva that runs the classes has mental glitter nails and she plays fantastic music and SCREAMS at you to dance in the water so you don't drown.'
Britannia Leisure Centre,
40 Hyde Road, N1 5JU

4 Skating

'Most nights in Stratford you can see the future of roller skating. These kids have modified sneakers into skates; they play music off their phones and never have their laces done up. They take advantage of the marble shopping-centre floors and skate real late.'
Stratford Centre, 54a Broadway, E15 1NG
http://stratfordshopping.co.uk

5 Tango Social

'A late-night Argentinian workout in East London. For the most romantic night on the dancefloor, this is the place to go. Learn steps or watch and learn from the balcony.'
The Old Cholmeley Boys Club, 68 Boleyn Road, N16 8JG
tango-social.com

Marawa at her hula school.

Ridley Road Market

Ridley Road never fails to surprise me—and I've been frequenting it for the last
15 years. It represents everything I love about the multicultural heritage of this city
and that coexistence in motion. The neighbourhood's ethnically varied population
is the result of over 100 years of migration. The East End originally became home
to Huguenot Jews who, in turn, handed it over to a Caribbean community and more
recently Turkish, Vietnamese and Polish settlers. All of these cultures combine on
Ridley Road, where I enjoy being in the cobbler's overhearing a two-way conversation
in colloquial Cockney and purring paced Patois.

　　　Whatever you've got planned for your dinner, all the ingredients are available
here, plus some potentially unidentifiable culinary curveballs to throw in the mix.
Check out Lorenzo Vitturi's beautiful photography project *Dalston Anatomy* for
Surrealist still-lifes and portraits of the market's inhabitants. Since the council's
clean-up and knock-down sweep for the 2012 Olympic Games, some of the area's edge
has been cleansed and given way to corporate coffee chains. For this reason I urge
you to visit Dalston to taste its real essence before it's sanitised. Grab a lahmacun
wrap with a side of rice, peas and plantain before a Michelin-starred fusion restaurant
outbids the bookies on the high street. Keep your ears peeled for the call to prayer
from the mosque over the reggae from the pirate radio stations. Cater for a barbeque
with a whole salmon and squid and stock up on enough avocados to make guacamole
for a week for under a quid.

51–63 Ridley Road, E8 2LH
ridleyroad.co.uk

The Meringue Girls' spectrum kisses.

F. Cooke's pie and mash shop.

The Flower Appreciation Society's flowers.

Broadway Market

Another market with a pie and mash shop at its core is Broadway. It developed around F. Cooke's eel shop, which served shepherds driving their flocks into the city. You would be forgiven for thinking that the shepherds haven't moved on over the last century, judging by the amount of bearded men in the area. However, that's just the local Lo-Fi (London Fields) fellas. For here we are in the epicentre of East London's trendy residential realm, which revived the market in 2004 after its disappearance in the 1980s.

Broadway Market is still not very accessible by public transport, but it's worth the walk for the coffee spots that have sprung up. My suggestion for the most unexpected but seriously best brunch is Little Georgia on Goldsmiths Row. This Georgian restaurant serves 'Chizzi Bizzi'—the bee's knees—or home-cooked baked beans with sausages and sexy scrambled eggs. You'll never have had anything like it before and won't be able to recreate it at home, which accounts for the number of bums on seats in this place.

Broadway Market, E8 4QL
broadwaymarket.co.uk

Brick Lane Market antiques.

Brick Lane Market

If you want to get totally submerged somewhere for a whole Sunday, it doesn't get better than Brick Lane. Start at Spitalfields Market (1) first, then tear yourself away to walk up Hanbury Street (2) for the total Old Truman Brewery experience (3), before dipping into Dray Walk (4). Continue on to Cheshire Street (5) and follow the flow further to Columbia Road (6) and, finally, double back up Bethnal Green Road (7). I would need a separate book to mention all of the doors you must explore on this trail, so you're just going to have to go it alone and have fun finding out for yourself! Here are some tips and pointers:

1) Spitalfields Market
The Victorian market hall is worth a wander through to see the skylit structure and stop for a spot of brunch at Canteen. Exit opposite Fournier Street to find the home of Gilbert & George and look around to pay homage to the heritage of the Huguenot weavers who were the first artisans to settle here.
Brushfield Street, E1 6AA
spitalfields.co.uk

2) Hanbury Street

Glance at the glowing neon of Tracey Emin's sculpture hanging in the Golden Heart pub on the corner. Absolute Vintage display their garms in spectrum-ordered rails and the Old Truman Brewery complex starts here with the Sunday Up market.

3) The Old Truman Brewery

I confess, I rarely enter this cavernous vortex because I can't cope with a labyrinth full of lost, meandering tourists. I dart down a rabbit-warren trapdoor to an underground second-hand record stall and exit again with stealth speed after I've scooped up some 7"s. However, if you're after street food, it has to be said that the Boiler House Food Hall has the world's cuisine under one roof: 30 stalls, to be precise, with a lounge bar seating area in the winter and a beer garden for the summer.

152 Brick Lane, E1 6RU

boilerhouse-foodhall.co.uk

The Old Truman Brewery.

4) Dray Walk
Dray Walk's pedestrianised road of pop-ups is always a hive of activity full of sample sales, temporary exhibitions and graduate art shows. It's got a good deep pavement for a cotch to woof your pizza slice and watch the world go by. It's a street style causeway, too, for crews wobbling around the Big Chill Bar and musos en route to Rough Trade East. Special mention must go to Café 1001, which was my very first hangout here in the days before they had a liquor licence, when a hash haze filled the balcony.

5) Cheshire Street
Cheshire Street is a contradiction: chancers illegally laying down blankets of clearance items versus trendy homeware boutiques. The best bit is the old boy banging out tunes on a piano pulled onto the street. My main motivation for rising early on the day of rest is to hit up the hangar of second-hand and antique stalls here for random props and nostalgic heirlooms. At the very end of the lane is Beyond Retro, bursting at the seams with well-selected vintage stuff for both boys and girls.

Brick Lane food stalls.

Columbia Road Flower Market takes place on Sunday mornings.

6) Columbia Road

Follow the path of people embracing swathes of flowers to Columbia Road.
Prepare to move at a (florally apt) snail's pace, unless you have the powers of Moses
to part the sea of shufflers clogging up this artery of Hackney's horticultural heart.
It's mandatory to sample the local Cockney flavour with a cone of cockles. Offer one up
to the fluffy cat that's usually asleep on the sun-hot tin roof of a blue Cortina. Allow
the hawkers to harass you into buying enough bunches of gladioli that you won't be
able to see your way out of there.
Columbia Road, E2 7RG
columbiaroad.info

To conclude my Sunday market mini-marathon, you can take either of two paths,
turning left or right on Bethnal Green Road. Left will in time bring you back to the
start, where you'll pass Flashback Records and end up in the Sclater Street region
of toot stalls. Or turn right to root out a Sunday roast at the Approach Gallery's pub
and rub shoulders with the photographer Wolfgang Tillmans over your lamb shoulder
and trimmings.

Lily Vanilli

While you're visiting Columbia Road, take a detour around the side of the stalls to sidestep into Lily Vanilli's deli for a pre- or post-flower fuel up. The blogger-turned-baker who built an empire on riding the crest of the cupcake revival wave now has premises in which to cook and entertain. Every weekend she serves up sensational seasonal themed cakes for the sweet toothed and pastries for savoury fans to enjoy.

Lily is a fearless creative known for cake innovation; she takes a scientific approach with her anatomy-inspired designs and bold combinations of ingredients. Come in to chomp on a gluten-free grapefruit, polenta, almond and fig cake and take away a box of truffles or her *Sweet Tooth* cookbook for a loved one. She's cooking up a storm in a teacup for the tourists coming to Columbia Road and rolling out slabs of seriously moreish cheese on toast for the Cockney traders.

6 The Courtyard, E2 7RG
lilyvanilli.com

Exmouth Market

We take for granted the notion of a 'gastro-pub'. In fact, a pub that only serves alcohol —a 'boozer'—is the oddity now. It was The Eagle public house in Farringdon that first put quality food on the menu and the rest is history. Opposite this renegade tavern is the regenerated scene of Exmouth Market, under the logo of the letters 'EX' and an emoji of a mouth. It's a pedestrianised street that has made the most of being a street food haven. There's Ghanaian stews, hot salt beef sandwiches and the most sought-after tapas treats from the stall outside the restaurant Moro.

Exmouth Market, EC1R 4QD

Whitecross Street

Whitecross Street is the latest street food destination to get a boost despite having been around for 150 years. It backs onto the Barbican and leads out to St Luke's church on Old Street, home of the London Symphony Orchestra. Local Shoreditch lunchers can dine al fresco in the church gardens and catch a downwind chorus from a woodwind practice. Go at the end of the week when the market is at maximum capacity, with 50 stalls to chose from. Finish with a coffee at Fix Café to see artist Camille Walala's optical interior design and magic murals.

Whitecross Street, EC1V 9AB

Leather Lane Market
Leather Lane, EC1N 7RJ

Bistrotheque

Up a cobbled pathway parallel to the hip gallery hub of Vyner Street is the restaurant Bistrotheque, which arrived near Broadway Market way ahead of the gentrification of Lo-Fi. That's what its owners David Waddington and Pablo Flack do: they detect an emerging scene and set up an institution for its future inhabitants to colonise. (Since then, the duo have followed up with Shrimpys in a disused petrol station at King's Cross and Hoi Polloi in the Ace Hotel.) Everything here is fun and flavourful, from the soft-shell crab burger to the cabaret show of East London's finest femmes, for real. If you go for weekend brunch you may witness resident pianist Xavior's classical rendition of pop hits.

23–27 Wadeson Street, E2 9DR
bistrotheque.com

Artist Prem Sahib's 2015 Christmas installation at Bistrotheque.

E Pellicci

When black cabbies aren't queueing around the block at Eurostar arrivals, they are fuelling up at London's cafés. The original 'Hackney carriage' drivers make up part of the bread and butter (pudding) of the city's early lunch covers, alongside builders, old age pensioners and hungover students. One such haunt, E Pellicci, is notorious for having been patronised by the Kray twins and has been awarded a Grade II listing from English Heritage for its 1946 marquetry interior. The Art Deco-inspired fittings surround Formica tables that are still waited on by the original Tuscan family who were part of the UK's boost in Italian coffee bars after World War II. These delis are my number one go-to. Never, ever take a sandwich from a Pret fridge when you can order the freshest, fluffiest roll filled with Mediterranean delicacies for half the price. E Pellicci is not only a culinary feast but a visual feast, and priceless for eavesdropping. Everyone knows each other, and everyone will soon know you after Nevio's warm welcome, interrogation and five-star service.

332 Bethnal Green Road, E2 0AG

Fish Central
149–155 Central Street, King Square, EC1V 8AP

Dalston Superstore

When visiting Dalston, look around and you're just as likely to see an internationally acclaimed musician as you are an internationally imported bowl of yam. This mix is exciting for a visitor but mildly terrifying for a local. The regeneration and sprawl is an unstoppable force that is changing the area's heritage. But one institution that I have to give praise to is the aptly and deceptively named Dalston Superstore, the very first recreational destination of its kind to open in the area. Now, there are more cafés per square foot than people to drink in them, but back in the day the only place you could get a coffee was bakery chain Greggs.

      Dalston Superstore put up its awning in an understated and sympathetic gesture with the aim of offering an alternative lifestyle space for the neighbourhood. Run by Dan Beaumont, Mikki Most and Dan Pope, it was carefully planned to be a calm and delicious diner by day, and an outrageously fun club for East London's LGBT revellers by night. The breakfast tables fold away into the walls and the bar becomes a stage for the master or mistress of ceremonies. For this reason it's disturbingly easy to start with salmon and scrambled eggs and accidentally stay all day, leaving under the cover of night.

      The space also acts as a gallery, with curated shows that support and inspire the local arts community. The majority of London's young fashion designers have their studios in E8, so it comes as no surprise to see one of them in here picking up the Wi-Fi or a flat white. Come to enjoy the beautiful airy sunlit space, which feels like a Lower East Side brasserie, and sit at the window to watch the world go by.

117 Kingsland High Street, E8 2PB
dalstonsuperstore.com

Voodoo Ray's

If you can see the NYC twist in the decor at Dalston Superstore then you will most definitely pick up on the Big Apple taste via a slice of pizza at Voodoo Ray's, also run by the Superstore crew. It's a formula that hasn't yet overtaken London but is perfectly placed on this stretch, which has become a nocturnal strip of nightclubs. For a guaranteed quality quick bite before hitting the owners' club downstairs, Dance Tunnel, this is the best eat-in-or-take-away in the area.

95 Kingsland High Street, E8 2PB
voodoorays.co.uk

The Towpath Café

No need to read the Sunday supplement of the broadsheet you've brought as you can eavesdrop on your fellow dining companions, who have probably written it. Tie up your spaniel and sit down for the most laid-back delivery of your eggs over-easy, like a Sunday morning.

36 De Beauvoir Crescent, N1 5SB

Brilliant Corners
470 Kingsland Road, E8 4AE
brilliantcornerslondon.co.uk

POND

POND, an alternative dining destination in E8, has filled the void for a fun and naughty night out, tiki style. If you can't sail your canoe up west for a Mai Tai at Trader Vic's, dock up in Dalston for their eight-rum version, plus a menu of Spam fries, poke pines and Kahlua pork with pineapple pickle.

Unit G2, Stamford Works, 3 Gillett Street, N16 8JH
pond-dalston.com

Beigel Bake

There's a constant London debate on the Brick Lane bagel issue, and the jury is out. You see, there are two rival neighbourhood bakeries next door to each other and each has a dedicated following who will not stray from their altar of dough. I'm going to tell you about the place on the right, Beigel Bake, because in my opinion this is the one. The other has the option of choosing your own filling, but Beigel Bake's premade classics are so good—if it ain't broke, don't fix it. The traditional choice is between smoked salmon and cream cheese and hot salt beef. (Make sure they've put in the pickle if you're going for the latter, as it's a 24-hour joint and sometimes they forget.) Team this with a tea so well-brewed the spoon stands still and, for a treat to follow, try the cheesecake, if you can cope with a second wallop of whey. Once you've waited in the queue, which snakes out of the door, you may need to use the loo. It's a walk through the ovens out to the back, so go ahead to have a behind-the-scenes snoop at the boiling and baking.

159 Brick Lane, E1 6SB

A Little of What You Fancy

Having picked up a loyal following as Dalston Superstore's first chef, owner Elaine Chalmers has since gone on to start her own venture. She's a bit of a legend on the East London landscape, so opening night here had more of the fashion industry in attendance than one of the British Fashion Council's receptions at No. 10. At A Little of What You Fancy, vegetable and fruit boxes are stacked up as both interior design and a display of the daily seasonal produce with which Elaine cooks. It serves unfussy British food in a concise, edited menu. You know it's going to be fresh as you see the steam rise from the open kitchen.

464 Kingsland Road, E8 4AE
alittleofwhatyoufancy.info

Top 5 Record Shops

Femi Adeyemi

'Femi'. Mention that name and it will be met with fondness. That's because Femi Adeyemi loves people, personalities and an exchange of dialogue. It's this passion for opinions and voices that led him to set up the community enterprise NTS, an online radio station. My days don't begin until I've tuned into NTS, where a network of co-conspirators have been hand-selected to programme the presenters. It's independent and representative, so caters to every taste, from field recordings to funk, footwork, football scores and opera. While you are in town pay attention to NTS's events schedule, which sees the station curating nights at galleries such as Tate Modern, the ICA and the National Gallery, festivals like Found, and parties for openings—not to mention their own notorious anniversary club nights.

The charismatic Femi is elusive because he's always in demand, so if you see him out, it's a sign that you've come to the right place. He'll be absorbed in deep conversation, calmly debating or warmly laughing. Here, I've asked for his top five record shops.

1 Flashback Records

'Very rarely do I go into a record shop these days and end up spending more than my allocated budget. I've learnt to get more disciplined with money the older I'm getting. Flashback is the exception though—there just always seems to be something extra in there that I spend money on.'
50 Essex Road, N1 8LR
flashback.co.uk

2 Eldica Records

'I learnt a lot from working in this shop and hanging out with the owner Andy eight or nine years ago. It's still the place to find some of the more random stuff.'
8 Bradbury Street, N16 8JN
eldica.co.uk

3 Do!! You!!! Records

'Run by one of my favourite DJs and NTS breakfast show host Charlie Bones —apart from the records it's worth a visit just to listen to one of Charlie's stories.'
Sky Shopping Centre, 137–139 Rye Lane, SE15 4ST
doyourecords.co.uk

4 Rat Records

'On the rare occasion I do make it across the river I have two stop-off points that I always visit: the 24-hour Caribbean restaurant on Old Kent Road and Rat Records.'
348 Camberwell New Rd, SE5 0RW
ratrecordsuk.net

5 Flashback Records (Hornsey)

'Slightly less well known than its other store—but stocks almost as many brilliant records. Always worth the trip.'
144 Crouch Hill, N8 9DX

Femi at Eldica Records.

Rough Trade East

From its origins as a little West London punk record shop set up as a place to hang out, Rough Trade is now transatlantic. The original Ladbroke Grove site, which opened in 1976, has spread to both East London and the East Coast of the US in New York, with a record label based between the two cities.

At its store in Brick Lane, the huge premises in the Old Truman Brewery are used as a live venue. Often, bands do in-store gigs to launch their albums for the fans who are first served in the morning and get a wristband for an evening show. There's something quite *Charlie and the Chocolate Factory* about that, especially on Record Store Day, an annual event which brings major headline acts to their stage. Be sure to check out their list of events and have a go in the black-and-white passport photo booth.

Dray Walk, Old Truman Brewery, 91 Brick Lane, E1 6QL
roughtrade.com

Love Vinyl
5 Pearson Street, E2 8JD
love-vinyl.net

Sister Ray
100 Shoreditch High Street, E1 6JQ
sisterray.co.uk

Kristina Records
44 Stoke Newington Road, N16 7XJ
kristinarecords.com

Vinyl Pimp
14 Felstead Street, E9 5LT
vinylpimp.co.uk

Mike's Record Shop
Unit 29–31, Indoor Market, 98–100
Wood Street, E17 3HX
e17woodstreet.co.uk/shop/mikes-record-shop
woodstreetindoormarket.co.uk/mikes-record-shop

Cosmos Records London
324D Hackney Road, E2 7AX

Kristina Records, Dalston.

Rough Trade East's stage for in-store gigs.

Vinyl Pimp, Hackney Wick.

Dear Susan Bicycles' colourful fixie at Look Mum No Hands!

Look Mum No Hands!

If you're fixated on fixies or a regular roadie, this is the one pit-stop shop for all cycling fanatics and budding mechanics. A café, bicycle workshop, bar and exhibition space are all under one roof. Events include film screenings (live coverage of Wiggins's record-breaking one-hour challenge) and speed dating for single speedsters. Craft beers, homemade cake, chainsets and cranks—they've got it all.

49 Old Street, EC1V 9HX
lookmumnohands.com

The London Bike Kitchen

Peace, love, unity and a place to fix your bike for free: I love everything about the London Bike Kitchen. The non-profit social enterprise is an open DIY workshop offering drop-ins where anyone can learn from mechanics and use their tool library. There's also a schedule of classes, and a repair and servicing option if you don't have time to do it yourself. Their MO is to help anyone from any background to become self-sufficient at bike maintenance, contributing to the greater bike culture community: exactly my kind of people, purpose and place.

28 Whitmore Road, N1 5QA
lbk.org.uk

Morning Gloryville

If you're in an East London café ordering a morning macchiato and your barista is sparkling with a face full of glitter, he's probably just got in from Morning Gloryville. Let me get this straight for you: it's raving in the early hours to BEGIN the day rather than ending the previous 48 hours you've already been awake. There are no gurning casualties gripping an empty can; instead, there are thrill-seekers getting high on exercise endorphins and sipping smoothies. It's about setting your alarm early to see the sunrise from a dancefloor of smiles, jumping about in unison to euphoric club classics. It's weekend abandonment transplanted to mid-week 'conscious clubbing' to the sound of 'Higher State of Consciousness'. This international initiative has invented dancing away hump-day blues to Basement Jaxx before you've been hit with an inbox of 'Red Alert' exclamation marks. The whole thing is almost a religious experience due to the hands-in-the-air congregation facing the altar of the DJ and shaking to the hypnotic beat. Here is the future of clubbing.

Oval Space, 29–32 The Oval, E2 9DT
Check the website for dates and other locations
morninggloryville.com

Cooldown massages at Morning Gloryville.

Work It

From handing out paper flyers and selling beer in brown paper bags, the Work It girls have built an R&B revival empire. It all began in a tiny sweaty club in Dalston called Visions Video Bar, where Sisqó videos flickered on the venue's TV screens. Kids who were only just born in the 1990s were queueing round the block to get in to get down to 'This is How We Do It'. Versace high-waisted jeans were synched with Moschino gold belts and crop-tops were emblazoned with lyrics from the promoters' merch line—'Keeping it Cute' became a tagline.

This scene hasn't since Sim Simma'd down and is still going strong in special locations across East London. The roster of talent has grown, with the girls starting an artists' management service to roll the party out to international dance festivals. Keep a (Lisa Left) eye on the Family Art Music circle to see where the next party is popping up and popping off. Valentine's, Notting Hill Carnival and their own birthday specials are the key dates in the diary.

Various locations
youworkit.co.uk

Work It girl Rosy Nicholas with a wall she painted at Miranda's Basement, Ace Hotel.

Mica Levi and Tirzah performing at a Boiler Room event at SHAPES, Hackney Wick.

Boiler Room

Boiler Room started out as a group of friends live streaming DJ sets during intimate, spontaneous gatherings just up the road from my studio in 2010. Fast forward a year or so and I knew something was up when I was on a trip to NYC with its co-founder Thristian and he was getting recognised on the streets. It has since turned into an international phenomenon, broadcasting from 65 cities around the world (and counting).

Watching the pioneering online platform's video broadcasts is like having a fly-on-the-wall view of your teenage bedroom when you lounged around, smoking out of the window, waiting for someone else to move off the bean bag — except the key difference between your own den's decks and these dudes is that their network, amassed from music industry connections, means that the selectors are key players and game changers.

In a self-fulfilling prophecy, the success of Boiler Room has propelled its pixellated transmissions from an underground niche to world domination. Their home base has scaled up, as has the demand for coveted guest list spots at their weekly sessions. If you want to go, just be sure to try and get in on a night while you're here in their home town. Or put it on in your hotel for your own party ... they could even be broadcasting in dressing gowns from a hotel room themselves!

Various locations
boilerroom.tv

James Lavelle of UNKLE DJing at NikeLab's Mo'Wax capsule collection launch.

NikeLab

I'm a fully signed-up follower of the Just Do It lifestyle. There's something intoxicating about the lure of the swoosh, especially with the elite store NikeLab. London's location —one of the world's six sites—is secreted away in the east, far from the central NikeTown. Nestled neatly into a railway arch, it has perfect protection from the elements for the die-hard fans who queue overnight to check out installations in its gallery space for the launch of each new collection and collaboration. The concept store's ergonomic interior lends itself to workouts, with a rubber compound floor made from upcycled sneaker soles. Disciples of sport—and not just design—can also sign up for free in-store activities. If you're a brainwashed sneaker freak like myself, then this is the holy temple of the crep cult.

Arches 477–478, Bateman's Row, EC2A 3LQ
nike.com/gb/en_gb/c/nikelab

LN-CC

LN-CC (Late Night Chameleon Cafe) is located on Shacklewell Lane, which I've also dubbed 'Fashion Street'. Here are the studios of many of London's trailblazing designers, and I have a little game with myself of guessing which brand an intern is working for by looking at their outfit when running up the road. In the basement of an old menswear factory and now currently HQ to Christopher Kane and Peter Jensen is LN-CC. The concept store was set up by ex-Oki-ni buyer John Skelton with award-winning interior design by art director Gary Card. To step inside this underground alternate dimension you will need to make an appointment. However, the welcome is very warm once you are inside, and a complimentary shot of mescal from their unique supplier might await you. In addition to the rails of Raf Simons and Rick Owens, the boutique contains a gallery space, bookshop and record concession.

18–24 Shacklewell Lane, E8 2EZ
ln-cc.com

Gary Card's interior design at LN-CC.

Rio

I think the most fitting film I saw here was a late-night screening of *Desperately Seeking Susan*: the action on screen camouflaged into the interior. The blue leopard-print carpet is the predominant feature of this theatre, which is an immaculate mash-up of elaborate Neoclassical and Art Deco refurb. The 1930s *Metropolis*-style exterior is intact and a beautifully blue-lit presence on Dalston's nocturnal landscape. Fancy dress is actively encouraged for these weekend nostalgia selections and competition can be rife, with boys and girls gunning for first prize for Madonna impersonation at an *In Bed With Madonna* screening. The Rio is a community concern, as it also hosts school parties and matinees. The café even has homemade cake! This is a true independent cinema with a carefully chosen weekly rotation of titles.

107 Kingsland High Street, E8 2PB
riocinema.org.uk

Geffrye Museum

I have it on good authority from my friend Will that the walled herb garden of the Geffrye Museum is an aromatically special place, especially if the wind wafts in your favour. The free-to-visit garden of Shoreditch's museum of the home contains a traditional herb garden with English scents such as rose, honeysuckle and lily. The mix of culinary and medicinal herbs attracts insects, butterflies, birds and bookworms. Leaf through pages and simultaneously inhale the fragrant high notes of flowers underfoot. When the gardens are closed in the winter months, there is a designated reading gallery inside, complete with Kate Malone's botanical ceramic sculpture.

136 Kingsland Road, E2 8EA
geffrye-museum.org

The Geffrye's Reading Room with a Kate Malone ceramic piece.

York Hall Day Spa

Another facet of East London's fascinating immigrant Jewish legacy is the Turkish baths and Russian sauna that now operate as a spa at York Hall in Bethnal Green. First opened in 1929, it now runs as a charitable social enterprise serving the community, offering spa facilities at an accessible price. It's the perfect place to go for special occasions when there's a large number of ladies or lads to treat, and is ideal for hen dos or birthdays. The recently refurbished spa baths also offer modern beauty treatments and massage therapies. It was once the site of a famous boxing ring, so you can bowl around the building in your robe and towel imagining you are an ace sparrer while in the spa ... or that might just be me, wiping the sweat from my brow as I hallucinate in the heat of the sauna.

York Hall Leisure Centre, Old Ford Road, E2 9PJ
spa-london.org/yorkhall

WAH Nails

Book an appointment with one of the WAH girls early to avoid disappointment, have your new designs photographed, and pick up one of their iridescent kit bags.

494 Kingsland Road, E8 4AE
wah-nails.com

Bleach

Bleach does exactly what it says on the tin. And then some. Here is a hairdresser's with a difference, conceived with wisdom in youth by founder Alex Brownsell in 2010 and now capturing the city's creative imagination. Formulas mixed in Brownsell's bathroom became a bona fide business, ultimately moving into the back of WAH's nail bar in Dalston. No longer is multicoloured hair associated with Camden's crusties; it's now the dream to resemble a coral-haired Kate Moss from a Juergen Teller photo. Keep your colour topped up in between visits with their takeaway pigment range.

420 Kingsland Road, E8 4AA
bleachlondon.co.uk

Top 5 Beauty Shops

Sharmadean Reid

It wouldn't be a London book without hailing the queen bee of beauty—Sharmadean Reid MBE (voted one of 15 people who will define the future of arts in Britain when she was 24). With a background in trend consultancy, in 2009 she had the insight to see a gap in the market for an emerging nail art phenomenon about to go mainstream. Using the branding of her fanzine *WAH!* she opened her own nail bar in Dalston and used the space for exhibitions and launches. The E8 premises has returned after a concession within the labyrinth of Oxford Circus' Topshop. Meanwhile, the empire has metamorphosed into a nail-care line on high-street chemists' shelves. The designs that Sharma invents for shows at fashion week or for her musician friends (M.I.A, fka Twigs) can now be reinterpreted by teenagers at home across the globe. I bet the teenage Sharma, who hails from Wolverhampton, would have been pleased as punch to know she would become one of her generation's leading entrepreneurs. She's a fountain of knowledge, a force of inspiration and a fun tornado of energy. Here, she divulges her top five London beauty shops.

1 John Bell & Croyden

'I love the Old-World-meets-New-World feel of this space. It truly is a global apothecary, yet it's completely modern and energised. All pharmacies and beauty stores should check their approach.'
50–54 Wigmore Street, W1U 2AU
johnbellcroyden.co.uk

2 Planet Organic

'The best selection of natural products. Because I believe health comes from the inside, I love that I can buy food which will nourish me as well as Dr Hauschka, REN, Wild Nutrition and all my other fave products.'
Multiple locations
planetorganic.com

3 Panacea Health & Beauty

'This little gem has all sorts of weird health products like slippery elm porridge … but I also love that, instead of taking a whole brand range, they will just feature cult products like my absolute fave Nubian Heritage African Black Soap body wash.'
99 Muswell Hill Broadway, N10 3RS

4 Baywood Chemist

'I just moved to West London and there are loads of great chemists there, but I really love this one. A mix of higgledy-piggledy deadstock products as well as luxury beauty brands—and it's on the most beaut part of the Grove.'
239 Westbourne Grove, W11 2SE

5 Liberty Beauty Hall

'For my luxury beauty, I always shop here. It's been my fave since I first moved to London. I love wooden spaces and I love the traditional feel. Although it can get quite crowded, I still go there at least once a week to buy and browse.'
Regent Street, W1B 5AH
liberty.co.uk

Sharmadean at WAH Nails.

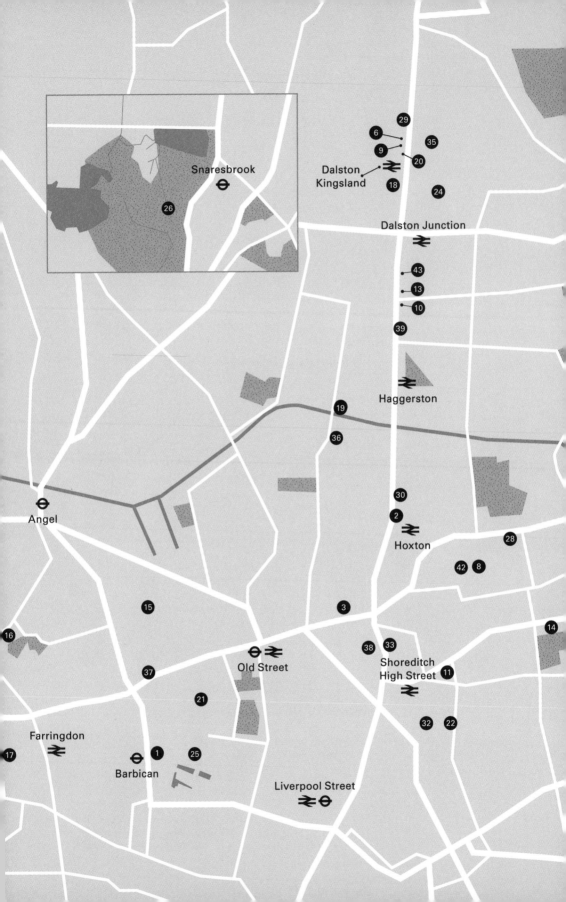

Snaresbrook

26

Dalston
Kingsland

6
29
9
35
20
18
24

Dalston Junction

43
13
10
39

Haggerston

19
36

30
2
Hoxton
28

42 8

3

15

16

14

38 33
Shoreditch
High Street
11

Old Street

37

21

32 22

Farringdon

17

1
25

Barbican

Angel

Liverpool Street

5

31

Wood Street
⇌

34

Hackney Wick
⇌

41

Walthamstow
Market
Ⓞ

ondon Fields
⇌

27

12

⇌

bridge
eath

44

4

Ⓞ

hnal Green

Zoe's Ghana Kitchen

Zoe Adjonyoh's contemporary take on Ghanaian food sees the cuisine reinvented to provide slow-cooked classics as quick snacks. The menu includes a grilled chicken jollof spiced burger, nkatenkwan wraps and garden egg moussaka with sweet dough bread. A full range of African drinks is also available, including African Fanta, malt beer, malt Guinness and palm wine. Her shipping container at Pop Brixton is putting Ghana on the pop-up food map. Pop in to try out her cosmic food cooked with love in a colourful interior she has handmade herself.

zoesghanakitchen.co.uk/restaurant

Pop Brixton's shipping containers designed by Eley Kishimoto.

Zoe's Ghana Kitchen's lamb and jollof rice.

Borough Market's wild mushrooms.

Borough Market

'London's larder' is a foodie's paradise and playground with 100 stalls of speciality traders. It's a mix of both groceries and gourmet street food, so you can do your weekend shop and simultaneously get your five-a-day in one go. If you're too brassic to be buying up the brassica, then take full advantage of the free samples. In theory, you can get away with a whole tasting menu if you circulate the complete coterie of cooked goods left out for the taking. Each business under the glass and ironwork roof has been recruited by a regulation committee — a panel of experts handpick the traders to maintain high standards and quality. Consider yourself a key contributor to this process as you poison-test each morsel of manchego and meringue.

8 Southwark Street, SE1 1TL
boroughmarket.org.uk

Scooter Caffè

London is the sartorial birthplace of so many significant subcultures that it's reassuring to see that traces of past genres are still upheld with each new generation. Scooter Caffè, behind Waterloo Station, is a time warp where you can get swept back to the heyday of 1950s and '60s coffee shops. Original Mods congregate here before they set off on an annual scooter rally out to the coast, lining the street of Lower Marsh with their many-mirrored bikes. Catch this spectacle for the ultimate British Mod experience or just pop in any day to be treated to a real one-off, authentic coffee made by a barista decked out in the Decca decade's threads.

132 Lower Marsh, SE1 7AE

Konditor & Cook

Most famous for its bespoke cakes that you can order as the best treat for your best friend's birthday.

22 Cornwall Road, SE1 8TW
konditorandcook.com

Rosie's Deli

During the rise of the blogger, Rosie put pen to paper with one hand and peeled and stirred pots and pans with the other. Now a published cookbook author, she has opened a second location in Peckham to compliment her flagship Brixton deli café. There's a counter of mix-and-match colourful cosmopolitan concoctions to both lunch on and learn from. Take away a digestif doggy bag and copies of her books *Supper with Rosie* and *Spooning with Rosie*.

14e Market Row, Brixton Market, SW9 8LD
28 Peckham Rye, SE15 4JR
rosiesdelicafe.com

Frank's Café

Frank's Café is an open-air BBQ and bar on the top floor of a multi-storey car park in Peckham. On paper, that sounds distinctly dicey. In reality, it's the most sought-after spot on a summer's eve and results in a constant queue down the concrete ramps. Just trust me and the rest of East London's trendies, who traverse across town to see the city from this southern panoramic viewpoint.

The bar was designed by Practice Architecture (Paloma Gormley and Lettice Drake) as the flagship architectural commission for the Bold Tendencies sculpture show in 2008; it was opened to serve the visiting art crowd with refreshments by bartender Frank Boxer (hence its name) and chef Michael Davies. It's been such a success that the drinks have overshadowed the installations, so be sure to pick up the list of works before you peruse the cocktail menu. After a couple of the killer negronis, make sure that you're about to sit down on one of Frank's stools and not a work of art.

10th Floor, Peckham Multi-Storey Car Park, 95a Rye Lane, SE15 4ST
frankscafe.org.uk

Franks Café's Campari cocktail.

Richard Wentworth's *Agora*, 2015.

Samuel Nias's *All the Colours of the Rainbow*, 2009.

Bold Tendencies

Bold Tendencies is an art show like no other and one that has to be experienced while seeing the city in summer. It's the brainchild of rising star Hannah Barry, who started out putting on shows for her friends who were at art school. From their squats and studios in South London, she has now established her own gallery and organises this separate non-profit show to encourage the local community to get to know the local artists and vice versa. In addition to the works integrated into the concrete floors, there's also an auditorium installed (previously made of straw bales) for performing arts. The private view opening night is guaranteed gridlock, with the city's emerging art scene coming out to see the sunset and have a Pimm's at Frank's.

Floors 7–10, 95a Rye Lane, SE15 4TG
boldtendencies.com

Detail from the exhibition 'Riviera Style: Resort and Swimwear since 1900', 2015.

Fashion & Textile Museum

The reason I wear colours is to combat the grey horizon of this city. I like to be a little rainbow of sunshine darting about the smoggy streets, inspiring smiles from the unsuspecting rat race. If you look beyond the high-rises you'll find another rainbow in the shadow of the Shard. Here, our pink-haired national treasure Zandra Rhodes planted a pocket of kaleidoscopic wonder with the coral-painted Fashion & Textile Museum. The Mexican architect Ricardo Legorreta designed Rhodes a complete complex, with a rainbow penthouse to live in, a printing studio to work in, and a gallery open to the public. Here's one postal address you can skim read, as you're not going to miss the tropical treat while walking down Bermondsey Street. You can take for granted the rows of wonderful restaurants and end up at the new White Cube gallery, but be sure to note that Rhodes, a trailblazing MBE who has been prolific from her punk roots to today, was the first here when it was still a dangerous dockside wasteland. Exhibitions showcase contemporary fashion, textiles and jewellery, with each having a cohesive theme. Special note: if you're studying textiles and are a fan of her unique legacy, you can apply for an internship and a chance to live in the building's student apartments.

83 Bermondsey Street, SE1 3XF
ftmlondon.org

Tate Modern
Bankside, SE1 9TG
tate.org.uk/visit/tate-modern

Horniman Museum & Gardens

This is perhaps a wild card recommendation, given its relatively inaccessible location and comparatively small-scale content, but that's the reason I rather like it. It's cute and it's got a local feel about it. You can tell regulars come here just to hang out in the café as much as enjoying the gardens. The Horniman is an anthropological museum, established when Frederick John Horniman opened his house to display his collection of objects and taxidermy. The building itself is designed in the Arts and Crafts style, with a huge cosmic totem pole at the entrance—a good indication of its exotic contents. Alongside the exhibits are an aquarium and natural history displays. The museum's most notorious fixture is the giant walrus, who has his own Twitter account! The animal was stuffed at a time before most taxidermists had ever witnessed a walrus alive, so his surplus wrinkly skin was stretched out to maximum elasticity, resulting in him being absolutely and inaccurately massive. So good! This and all the other flora and fauna examples on show are intended for up-close and hands-on interaction, making this museum my number one recommendation for a family destination outing.

100 London Road, SE23 3PQ
horniman.ac.uk

The famous overstuffed walrus is in the centre of the museum's main hall.

Southbank Centre

Something is going on at the Southbank Centre. Well, obviously. But what I mean is that somebody's got it exactly right. I keep ending up there—finding myself at concerts, culture festivals, Q&A film screenings, spoken-word slams, silent discos, a street food market. One night I nipped in late to use the loo and ended up dancing to an incredible Afrobeat DJ.

Arts for all is the motto here, both inside and outside the site, which is the largest centre for the arts in Europe. Created for the Festival of Britain in 1951, the complete equation comprises the Royal Festival Hall, Queen Elizabeth Hall, Hayward Gallery, Purcell Room, Poetry Library, Jubilee Gardens and Queen's Walk. In the Brutalist building of the Hayward Gallery is where you'll find the art exhibitions, always adventurous and innovative. More often than not the shows are interactive, making the most of the ginormous open-plan space.

For decades skaters have been making a pilgrimage to the undercroft of the Southbank Centre's Festival Wing, a holy plot of land colonised by their own community. The Brutalist style of the derelict commercial centre built in the 1960s has the perfect scooped surfaces, concrete coves and railings for spontaneity. In recent years, a forum (Long Live South Bank) was organised to save the space from redevelopment. They fortunately won the case—with a significant campaign of public backing—to turn the site into an 'asset of community value'.

Belvedere Road, SE1 8XX
southbankcentre.co.uk
llsb.com

PolyLester's 'Arcadia Grandview' peace pavilion, Festival of Love, 2015.

These slides were part of Carsten Höller's 'Decision' exhibition at the Hayward Gallery in 2015.

Lakwena's mural for the Africa Utopia festival, 2015.

Southbank Skate Park graffiti.

Top 5 Spoken Word Spots

James Massiah

The MC behind The A + The E (theaandthee.com) is this man, James Massiah. Like an actual messiah, his life's work entails delivering words to live by. 'Daencing', 'Spaeking', 'Naew Funk', and 'Quaer' are some of the different themes by which he categorises the spoken-word events he organizes. When he's not compering these jams, he's on the mic of his own radio shows or sitting on panel debates and committees. He's been captivating crowds around town since he was young, from early Bible readings at church to Shakespeare in English class at school. Combining this education with his ear for extracurricular rhymes from grime, he pens conscious, political, social narratives. His verse packs a powerful blow and it's this heavyweight wordplay that's garnered him a word-of-mouth audience. He quietly glides around town on a black pushbike, head-to-toe in black tones like a spoken-word ninja. He did, however, honour this colourful book with a tri-colour-trim jacket for his portrait. Conscientious to the last detail, that's James. Here are his top five spoken-word spots.

1 Steez

'Southeast London's under-25s host regular weed-infused jams at various plots across Lewisham and Southwark. Legendary status on a local level, reputable among London's young intelligentsia and a proving ground for the underground stars of the future. One Sunday a month, somewhere southeast, good vibes guaranteed.'
facebook.com/Welcometosteez

2 Born::free

'Belinda Zhawi and Chima Nsoedo collaborate on a monthly event focused on promoting the work of black writers, with notable exceptions that include the cream of London's literary fringe scene. Last Friday of the month at The Russet, Hackney—the only place to be.'

3 SPAEKING

'A monthly poetry night that I run on an ad hoc basis at various locations across the city (most often at the Bussey Building in Peckham). Currently I'm revamping the format, with a focus on pioneering the 'New Funk' style of poetry. It's on the first Sunday of the month.'

4 Brainchild

'Once a year, West Londoners Marina Blake, Jerome Toole and their band of brainchildren stake their claim for a piece of the London performance scene's proverbial pie! They host a regular festival outta town as well as hosting film screenings, workshops, performances and poetry nights at regular intervals throughout the year. Not to be missed!'
brainchildfestival.co.uk

5 Burn after Reading

'Ex-Barbican Young Poets have formed a group and host monthly readings in Covent Garden's Seven Dials. Poetry sessions include pieces offering a nod to some of the more classical styles, owing to the tutelage of one Jacob Sam-La Rose, but enough of a contemporary edge to whet the swords of those in search of a modern take on the form. Notable alumni include Harriett Creelman, Lewis Buxton, Amaal Said and Tyrone Lewis. Check 'em out!'
barpoetry.tumblr.com

James hosting his Næw Funk Brækfast Show at NTS Radio's headquarters.

Lionvibes

Lionvibes, originally named Altone Records in the 1980s and '90s, is the world's biggest retailer of original press reggae vinyl, and carries on the rich tradition of reggae shops in Brixton. It has a portrait hanging in memory of the shop's original founder, Alton Ellis.

98 Granville Arcade, SW9 8PR
lionvibes.com

Portrait of singer-songwriter Alton Ellis in Lionvibes, Brixton Village.

Rye Wax record shop, Peckham.

Music & Goods Exchange, Greenwich.

NTS morning show host Charlie Bones's record shop Do!! You!!!, Peckham.

Do!! You!!! Records
Sky Shopping Centre, 137–139 Rye Lane,
SE15 4ST
doyourecords.co.uk

Sacred Grooves
98 Friary Road, SE15 1PX

Rye Wax
Basement, The CLF Art Cafe,
133 Rye Lane, SE15 4ST
ryewax.com

YAM Records
11–14 Holdron's Arcade, 135a Rye Lane, SE15 4ST
youandmusic.net

Pure Vinyl
33–35 Reliance Arcade, Brixton, SW9 8JZ

Supertone Records
110 Acre Lane, SW2 5RA
supertonerecords.co.uk

Gramex
104 Lower Marsh (under Book Warehouse),
SE1 7AB
gramex.co.uk

JB's Records
108 Lower Marsh, SE1 7AB
jbsrecords.co.uk

Music & Goods Exchange
23 Greenwich Church Street, SE10 9BJ
mgeshops.com

The Book and Record Bar
20 Norwood High Street, SE27 9NR
thebookandrecordbar.net

Bambino
28–32 Church Road, SE19 2ET

Soul Brother
1 Keswick Road, SW15 2HL
soulbrother.com

Bussey Building

A 120-year-old multi-level warehouse space which has three floors for either one big club night of multiple rooms or separate promoters' nights.

133 Rye Lane, SE15 4RT
clfartcafe.org

Corsica Studios

If you want to lose a weekend down a dark warren of underground house, techno, disco, dubstep and bass rooms, this raw space has the best sound system. It's currently the capital's premier authentic alternative club, still flying the flag after the torrent of closures of its counterparts. Having celebrated its tenth year, Corsica is recognised and chosen by the industry for landmark events such as Ninja Tune's 25th anniversary and Eglo Records' legendary bank holiday weekenders. Within the intimate atmosphere between the arches you could come across Yasiin Bey at a piano in the corridor or accidentally get a peek at the adjacent salsa club.

4/5 Elephant Road, SE17 1LB
corsicastudios.com

Horse Meat Disco

I have spent the majority of my dancefloor days within the smoke machines and strobes of LGBT nights. Not only do they offer the best music and a ridiculously liberated, joyous crowd, but the dressing up beforehand is equally fun. London has a rich history of seminal clubbing scenes, especially for underground underdogs. Some accidentally found mainstream status, such as Steve Strange and the Blitz Kids in David Bowie's music video for 'Ashes to Ashes'. This electric diversity has flickered like a flame and attracted the magical moths of the world who have moved to the city, like Leigh Bowery, and in turn produced iconic artists such as choreographer Michael Clark.

The cycle of 'children' coming onto the scene and causing a stir with their invented characters keeps the landscape larger than life and ever-inventive. Horse Meat Disco has stood the test of time, providing a weekly Sunday-night safe haven to an old school crew and the newly curious. It's a family affair, with a rotation of DJs who take turns travelling the world and spreading the love with their in-demand enterprise. There's no shying away from these boys, either—the music alone gets you up on the podium or they physically point you out. The crowd is always a bit 'real' and ready to take off as they spin Cheryl Lynn's 'Got to Be Real'. From a bar in Vauxhall, to the airwaves of Rinse FM, to the Downlow Radio tent at Glastonbury Festival, HMD keep us on our toes and buying their annual albums.

Eagle London, 349 Kennington Lane, SE11 5QY
eaglelondon.com
twitter.com/horsemeatdisco

Amber Swallows wearing NOKI NHS with Gavino di Vino, Kalypso Bang and Babs Darling.

Top 5 Pound Shops

Julie Verhoeven

In her innate self-effacing style, Julie reckons that she draws because there's nothing else she can do. In fact, her life is a cosmos of creativity that constitutes an entire work of art in itself. One segment of that multicoloured spectrum is the paraphernalia which becomes props in her films and adorns her studio and home. If you have a weakness for stockpiling stationery from pound shops or a penchant for pink washing-up gloves, this is the retail therapy directory for you. In addition, this simply wouldn't be a colourful guide to the city without an entry from this glorious rainbow antidote to the seasonally grey metropolis.

1 Pricebusters

'Covers all bases: cheap great tat and practical DIY essentials and non-essentials. Stock changes regularly and never ceases to surprise me with oddities. I recently purchased the ugliest toothbrush/toothpaste holder on the planet for under a fiver.'
311 Elephant & Castle Shopping Centre, SE1 6TB

2 E T C General Store

'This is a tiny family-run shop full of life and warmth. Every day they do a new jolly and colourful piece of pavement art in front of the shop to house the overspill. Lovely to see colourful chalk on the grubby streets of SE5. The stock is generally pretty old, and all the better for it.'
Butterfly Walk, Denmark Hill, SE5 8RW

3 Jewellery stall (no name, halfway down on left, every day except Monday)

'This really is a true gem. The stallholder tends to concoct most of the pieces onsite. The stock is generally blingy, bright, bold, glam and unique. It never fails to excite me. I recently bought a sealed odds and sods bag for one pound, which to my joy contained a tray of coloured fur-ball rings.'
East Street Market, East Street, SE17

4 Tights stall

'This stall is full of wild and colourful tights, stockings, jazzy socks and large knickers. Ghetto minx meets Cynthia Payne. Fluorescent lace trim hold-ups were the most recent treat to behold.'
Ground Floor, Elephant & Castle Shopping Centre, SE1 6TB

5 Poundbusters

'It's a joy because it's an independent pound shop, pre-dating the ubiquitous Poundbusters chain. It's a mess; you have to really scrabble around but the old stock is worth hunting out. It excels in naff toilet accessories of the fluffy kind, which I have a weakness for.'
80 East Street, SE17 2DQ

Julie at her studio.

New Covent Garden Flower Market

Previously having worked in set design, I have spent my fair share of bloomin' time at New Covent Garden Flower Market. One time I shot a room full of peonies and wanted a range of tight to loose blooms, so had to stagger purchasing stems over consecutive days of the week. Though it can feel like the film *Groundhog Day* on dark winter mornings (note the 4 am opening time), it's a joyous treat to return here.

As the UK's largest flower market, it claims to have 'everything a florist needs under one roof'. If that requires stocking life-size decoy reindeer at Christmas, then so be it. I love all the surreal surplus props as well as the beautiful section of seashells. There's literally every conceivable type of conifer and greenery through to exotic *Anthurium*—and then replicas of all of these in the artificial selection. Potted orchids are so cheap it makes you want an immediate refund from all previous IKEA purchases. Oasis foam blocks come in all shapes and sizes for classical flower arrangements or endless vases are available for looser styles. It's open to the public so feel free to browse, but be aware it's a wholesale place and the vendors' tempers may be a whole less tolerant than you expect. Wrap up warm even in summer because the air is kept fresh for the flowers' sake, not yours. Remember prices are quoted without VAT, so tot up your totals as you stock up on glitter stag beetles and butterflies.

New Covent Garden Market, SW8 5BH
newcoventgardenmarket.com

Brixton Market

In addition to a street market of Afro-Caribbean produce are three arcades which have been rolled into one and renamed Brixton Village. Here, the vibe encompasses a 360-degree spectrum of world cuisine with its bustling bistros and cafés. The initiative of Lambeth Council has undergone criticism for diluting the area's heritage, but the distinct Caribbean flavour is still evident in the glorious red, gold and green wares on sale. This is also evident come August, when the Brixton Splash free street party is timed with Jamaican Independence Day. Windrush Square has a main stage for local musicians and the streets are lined with sound systems, steel pans and drums. Needless to say, I'm always in the middle having one of the most memorable days of my year.

Brixton Village, Reliance Arcade and Market Row
Coldharbour Lane, SW9 8LB
Electric Avenue, SW9 8JX
brixtonmarket.net
brixtonsplash.org

Deptford Market
Deptford High Street, SE8 3PR

Greenwich

Usually, I get on the DLR down to Greenwich solely to dig the crates at my favourite record store. Apparently there's some other stuff happening of interest here too, like the Royal Observatory, Planetarium, National Maritime Museum and *Cutty Sark* tea clipper. In all seriousness, though, this World Heritage Site is actually the namesake for the very second that you're reading this in. The Prime Meridian line runs through Greenwich, so you can literally stand with one foot in each hemisphere on the edge of average or 'mean' time. Come April you could also be standing at the starting line of the London Marathon. Lots of charity runs take place on this panoramic hill alongside walks and a nature trail. There's a world of creepy crawlies to catch and categorise on Queen Elizabeth's Oak, which is so old it dates back to before her Tudor reign. The Royal Observatory houses the UK's largest telescope, so you can switch from inspecting insects to stargazing out at the solar system in one fell swoop.

Blackheath Avenue, SE10 8XJ
visitgreenwich.org.uk

The Meridian Line in Greenwich.

The British clipper *Cutty Sark*.

Brockwell Lido

One of London's classic Art Deco outdoor swimming lidos.

Dulwich Road, SE24 0PA
fusion-lifestyle.com/centres/Brockwell_Lido

Tooting Bec Lido

Another of the city's Art Deco lidos, but this one is the largest freshwater open-air swimming pool in the UK.

Tooting Bec Road, SW16 1RU
placesforpeopleleisure.org/centres/tooting-bec-lido

British Film Institute

The South Bank is unquestionably the best stretch of London for a stroll on a sunny day. However, the prospect is not so enticing on a grey, rainy weekend, and this is where the BFI comes in. It offers not only a world of hyper-colour film but the cosiest bar on the strip. Massive sofas are the perfect place to curl up for a catch-up with mates and a mocha after a matinee. The BFI has deliberately made it a movie magnet to get the public in and encourage appreciation of UK and world cinema. You can either get engrossed in one of their themed festivals or go straight to the IMAX for the latest blockbuster. It's officially the largest screen in the UK, so it's the logical choice for those epic CGI fantasy adventure sequels.

Belvedere Road, SE1 8XT
bfi.org.uk

Ritzy

Outside Leicester Square are other significant multiplex cinemas, such as South London's Ritzy in Brixton. Built in 1910, it still features the original decor, and its left-wing heritage has become synonymous with its history of showing independent films. A mind-blowing example of that for me was sitting through a seven-hour screening of Matthew Barney's *The Cremaster Cycle* in sequence. The spot where you would usually encounter a pick 'n' mix was replaced with an installation of petroleum jelly and a pentagram of plasma screens.

Brixton Oval, Coldharbour Lane, SW2 1JG
picturehouses.co.uk/cinema/Ritzy_Picturehouse

Rooftop Film Club Peckham

Deckchairs, blankets and wireless headphones—on a rooftop in Peckham!

Bussey Building, 133 Rye Lane, SE15 4ST
rooftopfilmclub.com

Top 5 South London Treasure Trove

Zezi Ifore

Zezi cracks me up. Whether it's affectionately meditating on the quirks of the diaspora on her radio shows or mediating a topical panel debate, she holds her own—and has everyone else under her satirical spell. Earning her (adidas) stripes as one half of the DJ duo Coconut Twins and editor of *Super Super* back in the Nu-Rave era, she's still totally topical, keeping it 'jisty' at her Local or Palm Wine Club club nights. Her most used words, 'LIFE' and 'MOMENT', sum up how I feel about her definitive contribution to London's youth culture and creative commentary. She has the insight and the sharp wit to identify it, rationalise it, review it and break it down before you've overheard it being bantered around the back of the bus. Nothing makes me LOL more than an Ifore foray into the latest 'fashwarns'—be forewarned.

1 Deptford Market

'I've always been obsessed with seeing how far I could stretch a pound. And a nugget goes verrrrry far in Deptford. From flea markets to fruit and veg, African fabrics, '80s deadstock swimwear, giant gold hoops and funfair-style hot doughnuts, this is a real London market with trinkets, tat and everything in between. Celebrate your spoils like a local with pie 'n' mash at Manze's.' Deptford High Street, SE8 3PR

2 Battersea Car-boot Sale

'This might be the best car-boot sale in London simply because it's the only one I can still make even after dancing 'til lights on at Deviation the night before. You don't have to be an early bird to catch the worm here; some of my fave finds were snaffled 10 minutes before closing (at 5 pm), including Escada belts, Bally loafers and a trolley-load of rare magazines.' Harris Academy, Battersea Park Road, SW11 5AP

3 Pimlico

'The posh environs of Pimlico are perfect for classy treasure hunters. There's loads of charity shops full of well-heeled cast-offs including Fara, Oxfam and Trinity Hospice and my teenage haven: Retromania, the vintage dress-up box of dreams (don't sleep on the bargain rails outside)! On weekdays check out the Tachbrook Street Market for food and bric-a-brac and then hoof over to Horseferry Road to dip into the Cardinal Hume charity shop – my secret spot for amazing second-hand designer bargains.' Start at Retromania, 6 Upper Tachbrook Street, SW1V 1SH, and wander on

4 Nine Elms Sunday Market

'I've been going to this market since I was a kid and, decades later, it never disappoints. Moody Air Max's to Moroccan mint tea, shisha pipes to second-hand electronics, hoovers to healing crystals, this market has literally EVERYTHING UNDER THE SUN, and it's impossible to leave here empty-handed. Once you're done, stroll along the river and make a pit stop for lunch at another local treasure, the fabulous Brunswick House.' New Covent Garden Market, Nine Elms Lane, SW8 5AL

5 Lower Marsh

'A mini-village in the middle of London. Better than butcher, baker and candlestick-maker, it's got a deli, a pub, two craft shops, a Greggs, a charity shop, a library and way more. It's the epitome of the high/low mix that makes London amazing.' Lower Marsh, SE1 7AB

Zezi in Deptford.

South London quintet The Maccabees finish a UK tour at home for 3 sold-out nights at the Brixton Academy.

Brixton Academy

Every band aspires to seeing their name on the front of the Brixton Academy (officially the O2 Academy, Brixton). It's the largest capacity venue before you start filling stadiums; if you can fill it for a two-night stretch, it's extra kudos. Some established acts even prefer it to a stadium for the more intimate connection with their audience. Either way, you're winning here. The sloping floor ensures a decent view whatever your position or height. But even if you can't quite see Europe's largest fixed stage, you can admire the crazy ornate decoration of its faux-Venetian proscenium arch and ivy.

The Art Deco theatre was turned into a rock venue when it was bought for £1 from its brewery leaseholders by Simon Parkes in 1983. Brixton was only just recovering from the recent riots, so it started out promoting musicians who were willing to take a chance on a new venture in an unsettled district. This began with West Indian reggae and blossomed into recruiting acts from further afield, such as Fela Kuti, who flew in from Lagos. It was the first London location to host early hip hop pioneers like N.W.A., Run-D.M.C. and Public Enemy. This visionary attitude held strong into the 1980s, when they were the first venue to get a late licence to hold raves until 6 am at a time when illegal parties were being shut down. This constant flexibility to flow with the counterculture turned a derelict old cinema into a main attraction for mainstream music.

211 Stockwell Road, SW9 9SL
o2academybrixton.co.uk

Rivoli Ballroom

The Rivoli Ballroom is totally magic and will blow you away the first time you go. From then on you will keep recognising it in films and the spell will be slightly broken, because you'll feel as though you've lost your special place. It's the only remaining original untouched 1950s ballroom in London (well, untouched aside from the odd picture frame stolen by Goldsmiths students, who used to have their graduation ball here). It is as though you've stepped out of Doctor Who's TARDIS and gone back in time, especially on lindy hop revival nights, when a tank is parked outside. The sprung dance floor, ladies' powder room and bars with banquette seating make it the perfect setting for jitterbug parties. The ceiling is laden with large Chinese lanterns, glitter balls and prehistoric spotlight lamps with red gels. The walls are also red with velour padding and flocked wallpaper, panelled with gold gilt frames. It's a neoclassical meets exotic kitsch 1950s take on Art Deco with a truly authentic layer of vintage dust. Located way out in Crofton Park, it's only rarely used for gigs but, when it is, it's glorious. I went to see Florence & The Machine's 2009 performance here, which was suitably set in this shabby-chic grand dancehall. More recently Damon Albarn selected it for his first ever solo show debut, which really cemented it as a Londoner's best booking.

350 Brockley Road, SE4 2BY
therivoli.co.uk

Southwark

Southbank Centre

Waterloo

Elephant & Cas

Kennington

Victoria Station

Vauxhall

Oval

Battersea Park

Clapham North

Brixton

Clapham Common

Loughborou
Junction

Tooting Bec

Streatham Hill

West Norwood

Streatham

Portobello Road Antiques Market

As a teenager, I used to travel into London from Essex on a Saturday just to go to Portobello Road Market. Now, as a Londoner, I still revere it with the same excitement. The only thing that has changed is that I've replaced buying Bossa Nova mixtape cassettes from the Acid Jazz stall with digging crates in Honest Jon's record shop. In fact, music is how I navigate my weekend pilgrimage to Portobello. I start in the Music & Goods Exchange at Notting Hill Gate before making my way along the antiques trail to end up at Ladbroke Grove (via Rough Trade). It's also a bit of a busman's holiday, as I once worked in the Music & Goods Exchange. This involved repeated explanations that A) 'No, it isn't THE bookshop from the film *Notting Hill*' and, B) 'No, you didn't leave your wallet on the till.' I mention this as a word of warning: seriously watch where you put your valuables, as your body will be frisked by professional pickpockets in the crammed pavements of Portobello. It's the world's largest antiques market, chock-a-block with sightseers checking out the bric-a-brac. Originally the stomping ground for rag-and-bone men peddling their wares, it's now the place to pick up an original Pentax camera and plate of paella.

      Halfway along the road, the toot traders make way for the food market with hurdles of banana boxes set like traps for unsuspecting tourists. All fruit and veg is here for local weekly grocery shopping and world food caterers cook up warm takeaway meals. If vintage clothes are your bag, walk down the sides of the stalls, where boutiques are dotted in between cafés and shoe shops. Arrive at Portobello Road Market, where there is a dedicated square of rails heaving with retro wear.

Portobello Road, W10 5TA
portobelloroad.co.uk

The Grain Shop

Don't be confused by the bakery name or the sign outside for pizza: this is in fact
a vegetarian mecca serving a myriad of home-cooked dishes. It's a simple system,
with a choice of three differently sized boxes to choose from and a counter full of
dishes with which to mix and match your own medley. Ask for it open and you'll
fit in a few extras as they generously layer up a mountain of hearty, healthy comfort
food. The range covers cuisine from all over the world so, whatever your taste, they've
got it covered, from curry to chilli to macaroni cheese. Remember to pick out a pud,
as they bake the best range of sticky fruit slices, cakes and buns. In the summer you
can cross the road and dine al fresco on the square or, in winter, you can pop next
door to Café Mau Mau, who allow you in for free.

The Grain Shop, 269A Portobello Road, W11 1LR

Lucky 7

You have to go west to find an East Coast American diner and a menu that lists 'cwoffee'. This independent burger joint from restaurateur Tom Conran is one place where you can be sure of being served a patty that hasn't been unpacked from a production line. In fact the prime Aberdeen Angus chuck is just one divine detail on a menu that also includes breakfast buttermilk pancakes, sides of chilli cheese fries and banana splits. For me it's all about the malts, shakes and root beer floats.

127 Westbourne Park Road, W2 5QL
lucky7london.co.uk

Golborne Road Market

If you have somehow missed the myriad of mouthwatering food options along
Portobello Market, luckily you will end up at Golborne Road. Once upon a time known
as Little Morocco, it has—yep, you guessed it—a North African neighbourhood.
The first time I discovered it, I kicked myself for never having ventured just a few
steps further to have the world at my feet. There's a fleet of carts cooking up different
cuisine, from Caribbean jerk chicken to Moroccan fish, Middle Eastern falafel and
fresh-pressed juices. My recommendation is the Portuguese delicatessen Lisboa
Patisserie for a perch to enjoy a coffee and the best baked *pastel de nata* in town.
Any Golborne Row visit must include pocketing these pastries and, once, I even picked
up a 1970s sofa from the furniture stall outside. It's still going strong in my sitting
room and is the best spontaneous interior design purchase I've ever made!

Golborne Road, W10 5PA

Rellik

To find this gem of a vintage store, just follow the 1960s marker on the skyline, Trellick Tower on Golborne Road. Opposite the Brutalist high-rise is the equally institutional Rellik boutique, an Aladdin's cave of historical designer pieces. In the 1990s three Portobello Market stallholders gravitated towards each other, joined forces and took a chance on opening this abandoned shop up the road. They uprooted their weekend wares and transformed bare bricks and mortar into their own slice of sartorial heaven.

The space is divided into their three distinct signature-style-selected rails. Despite the segregated buying, the store is a one-stop retail experience for a loyal fan base. Once I encountered designer Duro Olowu and fashion icon Iris Apfel in town on an accessories safari and, another time, designer Kim Jones had called in on his birthday day trip from Paris. It's safe to say this is the fashion industry's favourite place to spend precious time picking up precious pieces.

8 Golborne Gardens, W10 5NW
relliklondon.co.uk

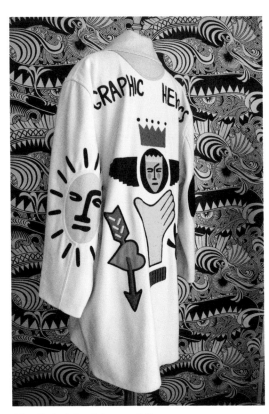

A Jean-Charles de Castelbajac coat at Rellik.

Notting Hill Carnival

One weekend a year, Londoners converge as one to reclaim the streets and pollute the air with deafening soca music and spicy jerk smoke with a seasoning of a sticky skunk aroma. Forget Christmas, this is the most fun you can possibly squeeze into a 72-hour national holiday. It's Europe's largest street festival and the absolute BEST celebration of our modern age of multiculturalism. Dreaming of its arrival coming nearer is the only thing that gets me through the dark winter months. The sheer volume of people out in force makes it totally liberating. This raw, frenetic energy could potentially tip into something out of control, but it's that fizzing excitement I bottle up in my memory bank as my own source of vitamin D.

Notting Hill Carnival initially came about from the local community taking action to strengthen relationships and support within their neighbourhood. There is debate over the actual year that the fete was founded; different versions of the story see it spread across three years. One of its seminal pioneers, Russell Henderson MBE, came to London from Trinidad in 1951 as a young jazz musician and started up The Russ Henderson Steel Band. In 1964 activist Rhaune Laslett held a children's pageant in Portobello and invited Russell's band to open the event. The players of the handheld pans started to walk to take the music along to the gathered crowds. This, as (one) legend has it, was the beginning of what we now know as the procession through the streets of Notting Hill.

Each year Carnival has a different theme and the various camps spend 365 days working on their garms, moves and sounds. On Sunday, mas bands pull out all the stops and bring out their cutest costumes for the Family Day Parade. It all culminates during Monday's main parade, when competition gets fierce for the final show and annual awards from the organising committee. Follow the trucks on the road from Westbourne Park station all along the winding W10 route. As you snake through these streets, shuffling and skanking to the sounds, you'll encounter 38 sound systems set up, including dub stalwarts Aba Shanti-I and Channel One. I love how the event brings people together, not just on the one weekend but over the course of the year it takes to organise the show. It's not just a party, it's part of London life, and is about inspiring the next generation to get involved.

Mo Flagz at the J'ouvert opening celebration.

Amira McCarthy in her Carnival Monday look.

Mahogany mas at Children's Day.

Top 5 Green Getaways

Sam McKnight

When he's not posting pics of his magnolias on social networks, Sam McKnight is picking up lifetime achievement awards for a career spent reshaping supermodels' hair. Chopping Agyness Deyn's blonde crop was a precursor to the revolution he started by heightening the fashion world's appreciation for flowers. With scissor hands and green fingers, Sam designs hair designs for couture shows and epic shoots, inspired by the blooms blossoming in his London garden. Who better to consult on the capital's hidden horticultural highlights and secret garden spaces?

1 Chelsea Physic Garden

'It's a true hidden gem, nestled behind high brick walls in the heart of Chelsea, and is packed with all the delights of an English garden, with wonderful knowledgeable gardeners who don't seem to mind me asking questions! And there is a great café/restaurant serving delicious food where you can look out for the rare (lesser-spotted these days) bouffant-haired grand ladies of Chelsea.'
66 Royal Hospital Road, SW3 4HS
chelseaphysicgarden.co.uk

2 Chiswick House and Gardens

'Just recently I visited Chiswick House to see their annual month-long camellia show, where not only can you view their fabulous camellias, many of which are centuries old, but they also have many of their beautiful specimens for sale. I bought three beauties. Built in 1729, the neo-Palladian house is as beautiful and carefully restored as the extensive gardens, lake and glasshouse. A real oasis where you can find peace, beauty, tea and scones just off the busy A4 to Heathrow.'
Burlington Lane, W4 2RP
chgt.org.uk

3 Kew Gardens

'A complete day out any time of the year —great restaurants, galleries, seasonal plantings, Victorian glasshouses and the vast bluebell woods in April and May.'
Kew, Richmond, Surrey, TW9 3AB
kew.org

4 Regent's Park

'The most tranquil, colourful and fragrant spot in Central London.'
Chester Road, NW1 4NR
royalparks.org.uk/parks/the-regents-park

5 Windsor Great Park

'The Savill Garden in Windsor Great Park has wonderful azaleas and rhododendrons in spring, herbaceous beds and roses in summer, plus a great café—and don't miss more azaleas in the nearby Punch Bowl.'
Wick Lane, Englefield Green, Surrey, TW20 0UU
windsorgreatpark.co.uk

Sam in his garden.

Richmond Park

You will probably have heard that Richmond Park is the place to go for a *Bambi* experience (but without the tears). That's because the nature reserve is home to a controlled herd of 630 red and fallow deer. The spotty fellas are everywhere and not shy of getting in the shot when you get your camera out. They've been darting around since Charles I established a deer park for his estate here in the 17th century. The oaks and other original trees are now key to the area's conservation. Within the ancient decaying wood is an ecosystem of fungi supporting a safe place for endangered species of beetles to scuttle round. Bright green parakeets fly around in formations like the Red (beaked) Arrows, adding more colour to the kite-flying sky. Birdwatching walks are recommended, along with regular park runs and a bike hire. My own experience of spotting the endearing deer here has been on day trips with my cycle crew. It's the perfect distance out of town to escape captivity and find freedom (like the parakeets).

Richmond
royalparks.org.uk/parks/richmond-park

Kew Gardens

Horticulture mysteriously seems to mainly be a pastime for senior citizens.
However, you don't need to be an allotment aficionado to appreciate the whole
lot of herbaceous flora and fauna at Kew, where landscaping styles from the 18th
to 20th centuries are showcased. Whether you're green to gardening or a green-
fingered pro, this UNESCO World Heritage Site is mind-blowing. Set aside a whole
day to wander around the topiary and botanical glasshouses of the grand palace's
grounds. In among the statues of mythical beasts are often sculptures by an artist
in residence, such as hand-blown glass swirls and bubbles by Dale Chihuly winding
round trees and floating on lily pads.

Take your own route through the tree borders to discover the ornamental
Oriental buildings and Herbarium. Head outside to get really high on the treetop
walkway (potentially not one for those with vertigo, but a high point for kids). Settle
back down to earth to tuck into a cream tea in the Orangery, then get stuck into
the succulents of the Princess Diana Conservatory and run around the Rhododendron
Dell. Don't miss the museum or Marianne North Gallery, with walls covered in her
floral studies from 1880s. I didn't discover this detail until about my third trip, so
be careful not to get lost in the world's largest collection of living plants and have
a good poke about.

Kew, Richmond, Surrey, TW9 3AB
kew.org

Bertrand Lavier's Fountain outside the Serpentine Galleries.

Serpentine Gallery

After retail therapy in the West End, wind your way further west for a dose of art therapy. A stone's throw past Marble Arch is the entrance to Hyde Park and a walk past Speaker's Corner through the glorious greenery will get you to the Serpentine. The galleries named after the adjacent snake-shaped lake are the sites of a previous tearoom and gunpowder store! Now the destination for acclaimed architecture, art and design shows, the galleries are five minutes' walk apart. The new Sackler Centre was designed by Zaha Hadid in 2013. If you're a fan of Hans Ulrich Obrist, try to join his 'Brutally Early Club'. The gallery's co-director loves his rituals and runs around Hyde Park and Kensington Gardens daily. In fact, 'Marathon' is the name he gave the festival they curate to coincide with Frieze Art Fair in October.

Serpentine Gallery: Kensington Gardens, W2 3XA
Serpentine Sackler Centre: West Carriage Drive, Kensington Gardens, W2 2AR
serpentinegalleries.org

Victoria & Albert Museum

If it's cold and rainy (highly likely in London, let's face it) and you fancy a day at the museums, the most obvious place is Museum Row. Here, you'll find the Natural History Museum, the Science Museum and the jewel in the crown: the Victoria & Albert Museum. Established in 1852 and named after Queen Victoria and Prince Albert, it has become the world's largest museum of decorative arts.

Between the halls of permanent displays there are always two or three outstanding temporary shows. The newly refurbished Fashion Gallery can be an immediate first stop, straight after the rotunda chandelier sculpture in the foyer. From the Japanese samurai helmets to the 1960s sci-fi furniture, you'll want to take it all home. To defuse this urge for illegal theft, the museum's gift shop is a sterling substitute. It's almost a gallery in its own right, with exquisitely selected contemporary covetable items from jewellery to commissioned exclusives (like my very own paper accessories kit).

Thank God the café is divine because, once inside this place, you're not going anywhere for quite a while. Between the 145 galleries spanning 5,000 years of art, you can take respite in the Morris Rooms restaurant. No ordinary canteen, the V&A's lunch hall is a ridiculously beautiful Arts and Crafts interior with floral repeat-pattern walls. Digest the zodiac-sign-bearing dado rails while you take time out for a cream tea. Here you will also find my favourite loos of the complex, so save yourself to spend a penny!

Cromwell Road, SW7 2RL
vam.ac.uk

A live event for 'Fashion in Motion: Kansai Yamamoto', 2013.

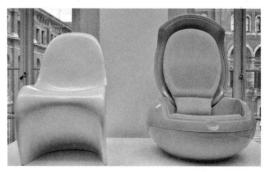

Contemporary Design Gallery at the V&A.

The Tabernacle

This former church is now a community centre for cultural arts and entertainment under the Carnival Village Trust. Right in the heart of the Notting Hill Carnival route is this designated spot dedicated to creating greater awareness of Carnival arts. This can be in the form of its Caribbean kitchen, gigs and shows in its theatre, or gallery space for exhibitions. Resident artists Mangrove offer steel pan classes alongside mas workshops. Activities span permanent courses from martial arts and singing calypso to temporary events such as playing your own vinyl on an original sound system. It's a home for all Carnival devotees who can't wait the 362 days of the year in between each August bank holiday. That'll be me!

34–35 Powis Square, W11 2AY
carnivalvillage.org.uk

Shepherd's Bush Empire
Shepherd's Bush Green, W12 8TT
o2shepherdsbushempire.co.uk

Bush Hall
310 Uxbridge Road, W12 7LJ
bushhallmusic.co.uk

Carl and Lyn Gabriel's *Carnival* garden sculpture.

Lloyd Coxsone at the 'Sound System Culture' exhibition, The Tabernacle, 2015.

Honest Jon's

The point of going to a record shop to dig through the crates as opposed to clicking away on Discogs is to enjoy the dusty-fingered panning for gold. One place that is guaranteed not to be a gamble is Honest Jon's—honest! Since 1974 it has been an anthropological pool of the world's rhythms and now, with Damon Albarn as part of the selection process, you know you're on fertile ground. If you're looking for a sound with soul, this is the spot, specialising in jazz, blues, reggae, dance, soul and outernational. I personally enjoy being a fly on the wall by eavesdropping on customers' banter as much as rooting through the Nigerian highlife section.

278 Portobello Road, W10 5TE
honestjons.com

Rough Trade
130 Talbot Road, W11 1JA
roughtrade.com

People's Sound Records
11 All Saints Road, W11 1HA
peoplessound.blogspot.co.uk

Music & Goods Exchange
38 Notting Hill Gate, W11 3HX
mgeshops.com

Top 5 Club Nights Of All Time

Benji B

North London born and bred BBC presenter and DJ Benji B still lives and works from his original ends. Although his social media accounts reflect his constant travel across time zones, his weekly Radio 1 show is a Thursday morning GMT fixture. He's played on the world's best sound systems and interviewed all of his own musical heroes along the way, which gives him an unrivalled encyclopaedic knowledge of the business. Benji's education began on the dancefloor of the Blue Note nightclub in its Metalheadz heyday and, here, he reflects on the seminal spaces that spawned what we now know as contemporary dance culture.

1 Metalheadz at the Blue Note

The Blue Note hosted nights by some of the best music people in the city. Metalheadz was the single most intense new music night I have ever experienced—the level of innovation was unparalleled, the genre was at its absolute peak and the vibe was unlike anything anywhere else. Favourite DJs included Fabio, Grooverider and Randall.

2 Balance at Plastic People

This small club developed whole genres of music and educated an entire generation on what great club environments can feel like. This is the space where I have been on the dancefloor—and played—more than anywhere else in the world. Balance, run by the owner Ade, represented the art of tune selection over everything else. It had various amazing guests, too many to mention.

3 That's How It Is at Bar Rumba

Bar Rumba hosted Gilles Peterson's night That's How It Is every Monday. It was an essential fixture that brought together different scenes and would often be packed until 3 am on a weekday night. I heard important records for the first time here, like brand new Carl Craig productions from Detroit alongside jazz, soul and Brazilian classics from the crates.

4 Full Cycle at The End

The End nightclub deserves a mention as it had one of the best sound systems in the world and hosted some classic sessions. Full Cycle's Roni Size, Krust, Die, Suv and MC Dynamite would come from Bristol once a month to represent their label. It was a magic, short period in London club life provided by non-Londoners and the energy was incredible, with tunes cut especially for that night.

5 Co-Op and FWD at the Velvet Rooms

The Velvet Rooms hosted legendary nights by Fabio and Carl Cox and new music nights Co-Op and FWD. Famously, both Co-Op and FWD moved to Plastic People after Velvet Rooms shut—but their initial sessions were very special due to the broken beat and dark garage scenes forming, the latter to become early dubstep. Both nights helped create genres of music and showed what can happen when DJs and producers have a progressive mentality to use the club system as the testing ground for new dubs. Favourite DJs included Dego, IG Culture, Seiji, Oris Jay, Youngsta and Zed Bias.

Benji B on the Regent's Canal towpath at King's Cross.

Equinox Gym

This international luxury fitness club has its UK venue in premises so steeped in cosmic club history that no other treadmill surrounding will quite compare once you know. When you're swooshing a sandbag into a rainbow slam at a Tabata class, you'll be knocked out to realise this was the original Rainbow Room. The Art Deco department store building was brought back to its original glamour under the brief rebranding from Biba in the 1970s. The top-floor restaurant and concert room's elliptical domed ceiling were illuminated in spectrum neon and seated a star-studded clientele such as Freddie Mercury, Mick and Bianca Jagger and David and Angie Bowie. Later, Bowie shot his *Jazzin' for Blue Jean* film here with director Julien Temple. That history—plus the Kiehl's products in the showers and peanut-butter-date shakes—make this my number one fave fitness hang out.

99 Kensington High Street, W8 5SA
equinox.com/clubs/london/kensington

The Conran Shop

Irrespective of personal taste, this complete lifestyle store is a contemporary treasure chest of items that you've never seen before. Surrounded by brilliant product design, you'll get a realisation that browsing to appreciate tactile objects totally negates scrolling through a screen of spiralling browser windows. You'll fill up your physical basket with things you've survived without before, but now can't imagine a future without.

Michelin House, 81 Fulham Road, SW3 6RD
conranshop.co.uk

Mathmos lava lamps.

Top 5 London Views

Zandra Rhodes

Fashion designer Dame Zandra Rhodes carved out a coral-pink piece of architectural history in London's evolution when she moved from Notting Hill to build the Fashion & Textile Museum in Bermondsey. The docks were brought into the 21st century and brightened up with this Mexican-style landmark, and the area has blossomed in the petal confetti falling from the rhododendrons on her roof. Zandra's swirly neon patterns and zest for life have been injecting refreshing, pioneering fun into Fashion Week and opera productions since her start in the punk scene in the 1970s. Now, she flies between homes in San Diego and London like a migrating tropical bird, chasing the sun's tail to where it casts most crisp. Luckily I managed to catch up with her at her spectrum-painted rainbow loft to find out her favourite local hues and haunts.

1 The Shard

'The dead area around London Bridge and its dark tunnels made SE1 a seemingly dangerous undeveloped area. People would look at the London Dungeons and say, "Sweeney Todd land—I'm not going there!" Then the magical Shard was built, turning this part of London into a focal point. Suddenly, restaurants have sprung up around the Fashion & Textile Museum. I have been asked to brighten and colour up the area—witness the Greenwood Theatre and its very special garden where you can sit. The area is now fab and thriving!'
32 London Bridge Street, SE1 9SG
the-shard.com

2 The Thames

'We are lucky to have this fabulous tidal river constantly changing the life of the city. Walk by its edges. Cross its bridges. Look at its ever-changing views!'
chgt.org.uk

3 Dennis Severs' House

'A national treasure and one of the most fabulous jewels in London. The most magical experience: a living "museum" that isn't a museum! Each candlelit room you walk into is as if the person who lived there has just got up and left. The powdered wig is on a wig stand. The fire screen is in front of the fire (to prevent one's face from going into red blotches!). The clay pipe lies by loose tobacco. The grand lady is entertaining on the first floor with her blue Delft china and with loose teas to be mixed (no teabags in those days) while her bedroom door is open and a chamber pot with yellow water is half seen under the bed.'
18 Folgate Street, E1 6BX
dennissevershouse.co.uk

4 Late night Friday at the V&A

'A wonderful Friday-night experience. Wander through the galleries cherry-picking the objects: a fabulous Turkish bowl, a pair of red medieval knitted socks, a plaster cast of Trajan's Column. The peace of the night is wonderful. Then, a band in the centre lobby entrance under the Chihuly chandelier.'
Cromwell Road, SW7 2RL
vam.ac.uk

5 Outdoor Cinema

'The films projected outside in the open at Trafalgar Square and at The Mayor's Office by Tower Bridge are wonderful. Last time I went they were giving out free raincoats, it's quite fabulous.'

Zandra in her rainbow penthouse above the Fashion & Textile Museum.

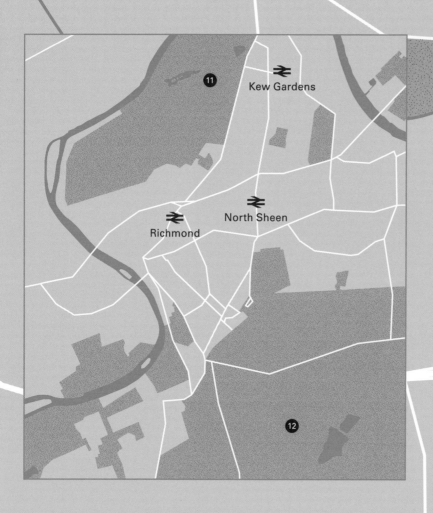

ART & CULTURE

CAFÉS

CARNIVAL

FOOD

MARKETS

MUSIC VENUES

OUTDOORS

RECORD STORES

SHOPPING

SPORT, HEALTH & BEAUTY

Shepherd's Bush
Market

Shepherd's Bush

Goldhawk Road

Maida Vale

Warwick Avenue

Westbourne Park

6

10

7

13

Ladbroke
Grove

15

4

Royal Oak

3

16

5

Paddington

Bayswater

Lancaster Gate

Queensway

14

Notting Hill Gate

18

Holland Park

1

19

High Street Kensington

2

South Kensington

17

UAL
NTS

JANUARY

London Art Fair

londonartfair.co.uk/visiting

FEBRUARY

London Fashion Week

Cambridge Circus turns into a circus
of the international fashion scene storming
the city to present next season's garms.
Worth visiting just to witness the street
style, even if you don't have a ticket.
Check out the events for the public at
London Fashion Weekend. Both events
happen again come September.

londonfashionweek.co.uk
londonfashionweekend.co.uk

Chinese New Year

London's central Chinatown welcomes
in the New Year with an opening ceremony
of acrobats, dancers and traditional dragon
and lion puppets creating a path of colour
across the West End. Head to Trafalgar
Square and the heart of Chinatown for more
performances and festivities, with craft
and food stalls.

chinatownlondon.org

MARCH

WOW: Women of the World Festival

To mark International Women's Day, WOW
is a festival of talks, debates, music, film and
comedy celebrating women, with incredible
guests. It was founded by Jude Kelly, artistic
director of the Southbank Centre.

wow.southbankcentre.co.uk

RCA Secret Postcards

Both established artists and Royal College
of Art graduates make miniature pieces for
an exhibition of concealed-identity artworks.
Register to view the exhibition and then wait
in line to purchase the postcards on a first-
come, first-served basis.

london.secret.rca.ac.uk

Peter Jensen's presentation 'Shirley' at Elms Lesters Painting Rooms with Bernstock Speirs headwear, 2016.

APRIL

London Marathon

Either follow the helicopter cameras from your couch via the BBC or follow the footsteps of the 26-mile-and-385-yard course to cheer the runners from the sideline. The route follows the Thames River, starting from Greenwich Park and ending at Buckingham Palace, with a street party for spectators at every pub along the way. Just like Carnival, it's a day when the whole city gets together to rejoice and celebrate this glorious capital, with Olympic athletes running alongside charity fundraisers.

virginmoneylondonmarathon.com

The W Project's Teo Connor at Run Dem Crew's London Marathon afterparty.

London Book Fair

Visit the book publishing trade fair and check the town's bookshops for associated programmes of events and debates.

londonbookfair.co.uk

Pick Me Up

London's annual graphic design and illustration showcase. Selected artists' works are exhibited for purchase and interactive workshops are held where anyone can get involved and get crafty.

pickmeuplondon.tumblr.com

Chrissie Abbott of Jaguar Shoes Collective's work at Pick Me Up.

Record Store Day

A day for international record stores to raise awareness and celebrate their culture. Staff, customers and musicians come together for in-store events and signings. Soho really pops off, with a stage erected on Berwick Street for a mini festival. Down the other end of the road, Sounds of the Universe put on a block party with a sound system on the pavement.

recordstoreday.co.uk

Record Store Day at Sounds of the Universe.

MAY

Chelsea Flower Show

The Royal Horticultural Society's flower show exhibits cutting-edge garden design, future trends and new plant premieres. Out-of-this-world installations are devised by leading landscape practitioners to win awards. It's key to sow the seeds of securing your spot by getting your tickets in advance for this packed out five-day spring show.

rhs.org.uk

My sleeve for Secret 7" on view at Somerset House.

Clerkenwell Design Week

Showroom events, pop-up exhibitions and special installations by leading UK and international brands in the design and architecture hub of Clerkenwell.

clerkenwelldesignweek.com

Secret 7"

A unique fundraising sale for all the vinyl junkies and art collectors out there. For Secret 7", seven tracks by historic and contemporary musicians are pressed 100 times onto 7" vinyl records. Illustrators and graphic designers from around the world then pick a track to interpret in their own style and create album artwork. The 700 sleeves are exhibited without description or title and bought as a gamble for £50 apiece, with the proceeds going to charity.

secret-7.com

Patternity for Paperless Post at Design Week.

JUNE

World Naked Bike Ride

I first came across this phenomenon when I left a hen do for a cigarette break to get away from the inflatable cocks, only to be confronted by a road full of real willies on two wheels. However, the World Naked Bike Ride is actually a serious protest event, raising awareness of issues like safety of cyclists on the road and reducing oil dependence. Remember that when you see the meat and two veg bouncing along the cobblestones of Covent Garden!

worldnakedbikeride.org

Taste of London

A five-day food festival in Regent's Park, granting direct access to top restaurants' recipes via chef demonstrations, master classes and tasting sessions.

london.tastefestivals.com

Art Car Boot Fair

In a kind of anti-establishment stand against the commercial practices of the art world, the Art Car Boot Fair has artists trading from their trunks. In East London, at the birthplace of the YBA scene, the community of artists set up fun folk-themed games and stalls. Peter Blake signs prints and Pam Hogg is on hand to part with precious archive pieces. It's an opportunity to get coconut shy with Tracey Emin and play hook a duck with Polly Morgan.

artcarbootfair.com

Molly Parkin's work at the Art Car Boot Fair.

Field Day Music Festival

East London's very own music festival, so no one has to leave the comfort of their own 'hood for a weekend's music in the mud. Since its beginnings in 2007 as a platform for underground and emerging talent, it's become a whole weekend that also takes on major headlining acts.

fielddayfestivals.com

Serpentine Pavilion

The Serpentine has an annual temporary pavilion commissioned out to a different architect each summer. Past names appointed include Frank Gehry, Ai Weiwei and Herzog & de Meuron, and Olafur Eliasson.

serpentinegalleries.org

2015's Serpentine Pavilion by SelgasCano.

Pride in London

On the nearest Saturday to the anniversary of 1969's Stonewall riots in New York, the streets of Soho become one united spectrum of rainbow flags, which pleases me no end! A parade takes place through Oxford Street and Regent Street, with a political rally after the main parade.

prideinlondon.org

JULY

Independent Label Market

In these days of download culture and collecting music at the click of a mouse, the Independent Label Market started up to reinstate physical purchasing's power. It began on Berwick Street Market (aka record shop row), with labels taking pitches on the market stalls to fill crates with the fruits of their labour. It's since scaled up to Spitalfields Market but maintained the gimmick, now teaming with craft breweries for a combined festival of beer and beats.

independentlabelmarket.com

Jazz Man Records's stall at the Independent Label Market.

Wimbledon Championships

When my aunt casually asked me if I'd like to go to Wimbledon one day, I had an inkling that I should go, as I had never had the opportunity before. Fast forward through a few hours of sipping Pimm's in the sun and we watched Andy Murray win the men's singles. I had no idea it was the day of the finals, and little did I know what a historic moment I would witness!

wimbledon.com

Hyper Japan

hyperjapan.co.uk

Beth Ditto at Lovebox.

Lovebox Music Festival

Founded by Groove Armada, Lovebox is indeed a line-up put together with love. With four days dedicated to different genres, there's a ticket for everyone.

loveboxfestival.com

Hyper Japan, a celebration of Japanese culture.

AUGUST

Meltdown Music Festival

The only meltdown you're going to have at this music festival is working out how many of the gigs you can feasibly go to. Each year the Southbank Centre invites a musician to curate the schedule of their favourite acts and events. This mantle has previously been taken by Yoko Ono, Massive Attack and David Byrne. I get totally over-excited and spend the majority of the time darting between talks, DJ sets and specially-orchestrated concerts. A lot of these activities are free, held in the concourse spaces of the Southbank, so it's well worth just hanging out to see what you can sneak into.

southbankcentre.co.uk

Notting Hill Carnival

thenottinghillcarnival.com

SEPTEMBER

Art Book Fair

Celebrating the best of international contemporary art publishing at the Whitechapel Gallery.

whitechapelgallery.org/events/london-art-book-fair

Open House

Festival to promote public awareness and appreciation for the capital's architecture by opening buildings up to public view. Check the programme each year to see which private establishments have put themselves up for invasion and scrutiny.

openhouselondon.org.uk

Pearly Kings & Queens Harvest Festival

You don't get much more of an archetypal London idiosyncrasy than the image of a Pearly Queen or King. Their annual Harvest Festival is an opportunity to see the whole community out in force, with all 30 families together. The original market traders, or 'costermongers', acquired their peculiar pearl-button adornment after taking inspiration from an early 19th-century fashion for wearing pearls. The contemporary characters are their direct descendants, who represent each borough of the city, with the names spelled out across the back of their embroidered Smother/Skeleton suits. Fundraising is at the heart of their inherited beliefs, and proceeds raised at the festival go to the homeless charities in the area. Donate to a good cause and get fantastic photos of the pearl-button-encrusted outfits and multicoloured ostrich-feather hats.

pearlysociety.co.uk

Pearly Kings & Queens Harvest Festival.

OCTOBER

London Film Festival

As London's answer to Cannes, the BFI's objective with this event is to screen titles that might not otherwise get UK exposure. All categories of motion picture are covered, from feature films to shorts and documentaries.

bfi.org.uk/lff

Cory Arcangel's work at Lisson Gallery's booth during Frieze Art Fair, 2015.

Frieze Art Fair

For a few days in October, London is the focus of the international art world, with collectors and advisors flying in to shop at Frieze Art Fair. The oldest art is housed in the Frieze Masters tent, which comprises dealers 'offering a contemporary lens on historical art'. The main arena has a space for every gallery to represent their artists, from the mighty sharks down to the small-fry start-ups. If you can't get into the show, make sure you take a walk around the adjacent sculpture park in Regent's Park, where 3D work can be viewed for free!

friezelondon.com

Diwali

Thanks to the mayor of London, once a year Trafalgar Square becomes a free concert for the festival of light, Diwali, celebrated by Hindus, Jains and Sikhs. Literally meaning 'row of lamps', it marks a new beginning, with light overshadowing dark representing good overcoming evil. Traditional religious music opens and closes the show, with contemporary Asian music, theatrics and dance displayed by different groups. There's also a multitude of creative activities to take part in, from storytelling to sari draping and face painting.

diwaliinlondon.com

NOVEMBER

MoRunning

Let your inner Mo Farah out at MoRunning by getting a moustache on to take part in this fun run to raise money and awareness for Prostate Cancer UK. The London division of this national event takes place at Greenwich Park, with a field of runners with stick-on moustaches marching up and down the hills for a great cause.

mo-running.com

Remembrance Sunday

On the second Sunday in November, the monarch leads the country in a day devoted to honouring the memories of those who have given their lives for peace and freedom. A wreath is laid at the Cenotaph in a ceremony that originally commemorated those who died in World War I, but now remembers all those who have been victims of conflict in service for their country. It's really important to donate to the great work of the British Legion and wear a red poppy with pride. Customize it with a sprinkle of red glitter for a cosmic touch!

britishlegion.org.uk

Fireworks for Guy Fawkes Night.

An operatic tree sound installation during Christmas at Kew.

Guy Fawkes Night

'Remember, remember the fifth of
November, the Gunpowder treason and
plot.' That's the history of fireworks night
succinctly outlined in one line of a nursery
rhyme. To explain the background of why
you find yourself spelling your name out
with a sparkler in one hand and keeping
a baked potato warm in your pocket with
the other, a guy called Guy attempted to
blow up the Houses of Parliament with his
fellow Catholic conspirators in 1605. The
felons were arrested, tortured and executed,
which is now bizarrely re-enacted by burning
an effigy of the poor 'guy' atop a bonfire.
The best bonfires to behold are a year in the
making at Lewes Bonfire Night in Sussex,
but if you are in London, numerous parks
put on firework displays that are a
pyromaniac's dream.

visitlondon.com/tag/bonfire-night

DECEMBER

Christmas at Kew

Ideally you want to see Kew in the daylight,
but December is the one exception to the
rule. The botanic gardens are illuminated
at Christmas with an after-dark experience.
A mile-long trail of artists' neon installations
light up the paths and glasshouse pavilions.

kew.org

Christmas Eve Carol Singing

Trafalgar Square at the Christmas tree.

Crisis at Christmas

Sign up to Crisis' volunteer scheme and
help run one of their centres offering safety,
warmth, washing facilities, food and
companionship for homeless people. You
never know, the sense of fulfilment from
helping others might just be the most
satisfying Christmas gift you will receive.

crisis.org.uk/pages/christmas.html

Index

ACKNOWLEDGEMENTS

Dedicated to my two-nanna, a Spitalfields foundling baby who found her way into the world on her own. To my family and its E17 East London roots. To the cosmically dressed Hindu girls I once saw driving a Lamborghini convertible down Walthamstow High Street. To Dalston, the East London that's been my base and the home of my best times. To its new generation who heard this whole project from inside the womb, Otis Abraham Ingham.

To East, West, South and North and the ashes of what once was, from the Astoria to Plastic People, from Mr Bongos to Haggle Vinyl, from Cranks to Beetroot. For vegetarian eatery Food for Thought, and the fact I blubbered and bawled my eyes out when I found out it had gone. To my studio desk where I had that cry, wrote this book and had to give up to make way for higher rents. To Charlie Bones on my radio every morning soundtracking these words and keeping me in check with E8.

To my parents and friends for giving me faith. For the time I answered the phone to my dad during the Changing of the Guard at Buckingham Palace and assured him I was at work. To the cocktail bars who poured me Long Island iced teas long before tea, and I assured them it was for work.

To all the contributors who generously gave me their time to peek into their worlds; I'll treasure it forever. To Charlie Dark, who saved my life, although he doesn't know it. (And to that end, the reason this book has its title.) To Tara Darby who joined on me on this odyssey during her own life-creation journey. And, last but not least to where it all began, Ali Gitlow—the world's best Lazy Oaf ambassador and book commissioner. Thank you.

Thank you every single peek of sunshine, person, postcode, moment and memory. London, I LOVE YOU.

AUTHOR BIOGRAPHY

Fred Butler is a London-based creative known for occupying the space between fashion, art and craft. Her blog Fred Butler Style has become a spotlight on London's artistic community. As well as showing her pioneering accessory collections and fashion films during London Fashion Week, she has created iconic pieces for some of the 21st century's biggest names, including Lady Gaga, Björk, Nicki Minaj, Beth Ditto and Patrick Wolf. A unique approach to colour and shape has led to prop styling and set design projects for the likes of *Vogue Italia*, the *Sunday Times Style* magazine and Selfridges. Her many collaborations have included some of the world's best-loved brands, from Swatch and Nike to Barbie and Red Bull.

© Prestel Verlag, Munich · London · New York, 2016
© for the text by Fred Butler, 2016
© for the images by Fred Butler; except © for the cover,
contributors' portraits and chapter divider images by Tara Darby, 2016

Cover: shot in front of artist Lakwena's mural at Frame gym in Shoreditch, East London.
Hair by Fudge, makeup by Kim Plotel.

Prestel Verlag, Munich
A member of Verlagsgruppe Random House GmbH

Prestel Verlag
Neumarkter Strasse 28
81673 Munich
Tel. +49 (0)89 4136-0
Fax +49 (0)89 4136-2335

www.prestel.de

Prestel Publishing Ltd.
14–17 Wells Street
London W1T 3PD
Tel. +44 (0)20 7323-5004
Fax +44 (0)20 7323-0271

Prestel Publishing
900 Broadway, Suite 603
New York, NY 10003
Tel. +1 (212) 995-2720
Fax +1 (212) 995-2733

www.prestel.com

Library of Congress Control Number: 2016937249

British Library Cataloguing-in-Publication Data: a catalogue record for this book is available
from the British Library; Deutsche Nationalbibliothek holds a record of this publication
in the Deutsche Nationalbibliografie; detailed bibliographical data can be found under: dnb.d-nb.de

Prestel books are available worldwide. Please contact your nearest bookseller or one
of the above addresses for information concerning your local distributor.

Editorial direction: Ali Gitlow
Copyediting and proofreading: Martha Jay
Design and layout: Praline
Production: Friederike Schirge
Origination: Reproline Mediateam
Printing and binding: TBB a.s., Banská Bystrica
Paper: Tauro

Verlagsgruppe Random House FSC® N001967
Printed in Slovakia

ISBN 978-3-7913-8166-4